Management Clinic

(*A Chat with Non-Academic Business Executives and Owners*)

By: Hassan Imani

Translated by: Pitter Silone

Edited by: Majid Jafari Aghdam

Title:	Management Clinic
Subtitle:	A Chat with Non-Academic Business Executives and Owners
Author:	Hassan Imani
Translator:	Pitter Silone
Editor:	Majid Jafari Aghdam
Publisher:	American Academic Research
ISBN:	978-1947464094

Addressing my dear sons, Mohsen, Amir Ali and Mohammad Ali

The book you hold in your hand is the result of many years of sweat, study, research, debate and rendezvous with "business owners, senior executives in the private and public sectors, middle managers, employers, self-made rich people, as well as risk-taking and successful people; who, however, have experienced many defeats and victories.

Consequently, behind every paragraph and every line of this book lies a precious experience that contains an instructive memo for the individuals who scheme proposals and outlooks for their work life. (Even quotes from distinguished people have been included in the text).

I hope this book will be an appreciated flair and memento from me to you dear reader, so by taking pro of its innards, you will have a more fruitful recital in the commercial and managing world.

This is a "gift" presented to you,

Hassan Imani
Summer 2019

As an Iranian, I thank *Jim Ran* for changing the mindset of many people for the better. *Jim Ran* is no longer with us, but every single sentence of this mentor has changed the lives of many. *Jim Ran* was a top entrepreneur and a great motivational speaker. His work had a direct influence on the creation and expansion of other people in their individual development.

I am proud to say that *Anthony Robbins' books* have magnificently changed my life. This prominent speaker, by all means, calls for human progress and fundamental changes in their thinking. He is trying to attract people's assistance to make the world a better place to live. I dedicate this book to this insightful man with all my heart and wish to meet him someday.

Another prominent author and speaker are *John C. Maxwell*, who has written lasting works on leadership. Works that are among the best-selling books in the world. Day in and day out, I have read and recorded the major points of the works of this great man. I dare say that I have read all of his books and learned a lot. I dedicate this book to *John Maxwell* whose valuable statements shine like a brilliant gem in this book.

Spencer Johnson, who wrote a book titled Peaks and Valleys, offers many practical solutions to managers and I should acknowledge and express my appreciation to him. This book is dedicated to him with love.

The book Time Management by *James Menctilo* is also a unique work. This book taught me many lessons. The present book is dedicated to dear James.

Dear madam *Catherine Ponder*, by writing the magical book Law of Empowerment has created a great change in the minds of seekers of success. This intellectual lady will always be remembered. In her books, there are precious statements that I believe are an example of the most unique interpretations of life from a human viewpoint. I thank this dear lady as well and dedicate this book to her.

It is no secret that *Peter Drucker* was the most prominent theoretician in the management world. *Drucker* spent more than seventy years of his life to systematically review the management science. He was the father of modern business and is always remembered for his greatness. This book is dedicated to *Peter Drucker*.

Let's get to *Philip Cutler*. An unmatched master of marketing and management knowledge. I am proud to say that I have read some of his books and learned many lessons. I dedicate this book to this great man with all my heart.

Christopher Voos, head of the powerful Black Swan business group and author of world bestselling books on complex and difficult negotiations. *Voos* is also the author of the best-selling book of the year 2017, which has presented innovative solutions in the field of learning and complicated negotiation methods. I am proud to say that I have learned many lessons by attending his training classes. This book is proudly presented to him.

Finally, I dedicate this book to the great man of change, Mr. *Bill Gates*, the owner of Microsoft Corporation, and the technology man, Mr. *Jeff Bezos*, the founder of Amazon website, as well as the insightful man, Mr. *Warren Buffett*, CEO of Berkshire Hathaway Co., whose precious statements contain many lessons for us.

Hassan Imani
December 2019

CONTENTS

Preface 1
Foreword 3
Starting Point 5
Goal 7
Basic tools 9
Visualization 11
Pathway determination 15
What do we want? 17
To make a wish 21
List of goals 25
Financial goals 27
Business goals 29
Goals and others 33
Element of commitment 37
Let's be committed 41

Commitment, consistency of personality 45
Commitment in line with the responsibility 47
Accountability 51
Division of responsibility 53
Big responsibilities 57
Body and reason 61
The rich mind 65
The gravity of the mind 69
Power of thought 73
Understanding the work 77
About Dell Inc 79
Good feeling 81
Good life 85
Special people 89
Future Generations 93
Thankfulness 97
Power of belief 101
Competencies 105
Individual power, collective power 109
Reliance 113
Willpower 115
Inner force 119
Serious determination 121
Self-esteem 125

The ruler – the ruled	129
Manager's price	135
Force of the universe	137
Thoughtfulness	141
Decision-making	145
Receipt and delivery	149
Procrastination	153
Decisiveness	157
The plan, a must	161
Creating a foundation	165
Organizing	169
Brief and helpful	173
Marginal functions	177
Discipline	181
Idea and plan	185
Work lesson	191
Conformance between goal and plan	195
Conformance of goal and plan *(Another look)*	199
Time	203
Working hours	207
Time management	211
"Pareto Principle"	213
Priorities of time	215
Punctuality	219

PREFACE

One cannot exhaust the topic of "management" and its methods in a few paragraphs. "Management" is a broad topic and there are many different angles to explore it. "Management" is the most important and influential part of any organization and establishment. Undoubtedly, richer, wiser and more practical management based on the knowledge will create an organization with a strong structure, an institution that can carry out executive affairs with authority in the highest organizational levels and the middle and lower levels of the organization.

Management may influence an organization and establishment in various ways. One aspect is "action". A strong manager is a manager who can implement his decisions and plans. More than eighty percent of managers have the first say in defining the strategy, planning, and decision-making and they are masters at this stage but when it comes to taking action, they are incapable of it! Now, the reason for their incapacity to act can be debated.

Another type of management's influence on the organization can be "innovation and creativity". The most motivating element in an organization's transcendence is an element implying innovation and attraction, and no attraction is better than creating a new strategy for the organization.

Personnel in an organization get trapped in daily routine challenges when no innovations or creativity are observable in the process of executive administration. Think about how inventive and creative we are in our work as a manager? Have we acted in such a way that the human resources of our organization come to the workplace every day excited about new designs, new ideas, and new teachings, or simply by habit and systematic determinism?

If it is supposed to be based on antiquated bureaucratic habits and determinism, a lot of opportunities would go waste. Now, let's multiply the time wasted by one person per day into wastage by hundreds of people in the organization! In your opinion, is it not funny to talk about growth in that case? Another way of management influence on the organization is "time awareness". How much do we manage our own time? How can a manager who does not have management over time might understand the value of time? When does one realize that his organization's progress is being evaluated over time? In the business world, those competitors have the first say that makes the most of their time. Where is the place of our management in this game? Are we lagging behind competitors or are we ahead of our rivals?

The influence of management on the organization has many elements that are beyond this book, but if you are interested in learning more about the various elements in this field, I suggest you earmark the book "Management Clinic" as a must-read.

FOREWORD

The book "Management Clinic" is a non-academic book with instructive, energetic, and practical material that can certainly work in the field of management. The book's narrative has roots in studies, research, work experience in the business world, and the result of executive interactions and ongoing author's meetings with big business executives and owners. What is clear is that all the topics and practical tips of the "Management Clinic" have come from an experienced and skilled mind. Whether they are reflections penned by the author or excerpts from the great people in the world of management and other successful people.

That same experience and skill is itself a value and a capital asset that contains practical management solutions. Many successful people in the world believe that the more knowledgeable and up-to-date managers are, with broader vision and insights based on goal setting, planning, diligence, and taking action; their success is more obvious. Such managers are great mentors in the business world. The purpose of the book "Management Clinic" is presenting an instructional and practical content to engage the minds of executives with transcendental factors.

This empirical book seeks to design a successful career path for executives. It is going to provide managers with several ways to effectively exploit situations.

This book seeks to present managers with the best options and the most value-effective factors. We hope that the mangers who put their hands on this book will take full advantage of the book's most wholesome and most detailed content in it.

Lastly, the purpose of writing this non-academic book is simply to "infuse transcendence in the field of business management", which has been one of the author's concerns for many years. In advance, I wish to thank the executives who contributed to the development of this book by sharing their valuable experiences with the author. I also wish to express my special thanks to my dear friend, Mr. Ahmad Dowlatabadi, the great author, who could finally get this book published with a huge effort.

Hassan Imani - Spring 2019

STARTING POINT

The "Starting Point" is the spark that takes shape before designing a target. One day, one of the world's leading writers and lecturers was asked a question by a reporter at the exit after his speech ended:

- "How did you begin to become successful?"

The speaker replied immediately:

- "The starting point of my success was four questions: *Why? Why not? Why not you?* and *Why not now?*"

Success depends on the starting point.

For a writer to write a novel, he must first set his purpose and put two principles on his agenda:

1- From which point to start . . . 2 - At which point to finish . . .

John C. Maxwell states in his book *Failure is the Beginning of Victory*:

"... *You should start the work to find the feeling you want. Not just sit like a duck until the insight comes to you and encourage you to do something.*"

The starting point can be a simple statement. It might suddenly pop up in a nonprofessional's mind. It can come from a heartfelt faith and belief. The starting point can start at any point you can imagine.

Jim Ran says:

"The starting point can come from anywhere and from any perspective."

... You must think to find out where your starting point was.

The victors are people who take the starting point seriously.

Remember, even the most beautiful carpets in the world start and end with a thread of thousands of threads. To start any task, think about the carpet.

Has this feeling come to you yet?

The initial point sometimes frequently knocks on the door, but it is not possible to get all the starting points to the desired fallouts. Starting points fillip us. They nudge us to rise. Nevertheless, many people do not take such a starting point seriously. For a successful manager, every starting point contains success.

An intelligent manager knows that achieving success necessitates sustainability. The smart manager knows that not every starting point is going to achieve the desired results. However, the most important characteristic of an efficacious manager is that he takes the starting points seriously and certainly, this thoughtful perspective is very good and worthwhile. Taking seriously every spark in the business world is about taking victory seriously.

GOAL

It is better than in the first step of the business to engage ourselves with the goal. The profitability of this assignation is high. Do not hesitation it. Somewhere I read:

"All fruitful people were extremely goal-oriented."

Take this message seriously, if you want to prosper.

There is a purpose in our creation.

We all have the ability to have a purpose in our lives. Why determination?

Because purpose makes us much more treasured than what we have achieved. Because it helps us overcome transient obstacles in life. Now let's be a bit more serious ...

You, dear Manager!

Do you have a explicit goal? Where is that goal? Have you recorded that goal in the layers of your mind? Have you carved it out in your heart? Have you written that goal on paper or put it under your desk glass cover?

If your organization does not have a goalmouth, shut it down right now. This is the most serious thing I have ever said.

Wayne Dyer says:

"Constantly emphasize in your thoughts that you have a purpose in this world."

You define it ...

Some have goals but do not move. Also, some move but have no purpose. Successful people are satisfied to be paralyzed, deaf and blind, but not to be like these two groups. How about you dear manager?

Set your goals since undoubtedly the goals of your organization will take outline around it. Your micro goals will shape a large part of your overall macro organizational goals. Think of your goals piece by piece, without which the puzzle of your success will be inadequate.

Never underestimate such small goals. Just as a brick affects the strength and shape of a building, a small goal is also effective in building your success.

One day someone was lost in the desert. A passerby came to him and asked:

- "where are you going?"

The person answered:

- "I do not know!"

The passerby said:

- "So, any way you go is the right one!"

We need to know what our ultimate goal and destination are to find the exit to its highway. The nethermost line is that by the same total that your family, parents, spouse, friends, and relatives prerequisite courtesy, your goals are worth paying attention to (and perhaps more so).

BASIC TOOLS

You certainly know that every edifice, every system, and every purpose needs tools. It is unbearable to grasp goals deprived of tools.

The greater the intricacy of the bull's eye, the more tools are needed.

Somewhere I read . . . A 10- or 12-year-old English boy made a thriving business online by selling marbles. What do you think were the tools of this teenage boy? What tools did Lumière brothers use to achieve the dream of flight that could make a huge difference in the world?

They have no doubt dreamed of flying before.

The first type of basic tools for achieving the goal is "visualization". As a molecule has two or more atoms, the atom is made up of a central nucleus containing a neutron and a proton. So, the goal needs more details too. Basic tools are the most basic requirements of a goal. By putting together such basic tools, we can come up with a solid, practical structure that will help us achieve our goals.

Picture you have a white paper in front of you and someone

asks you to paint on it. Your mind automatically and unconsciously scrolls through images of nature, geometric shapes, objects, or other things and decides to paint something after an analysis of your capabilities. This browsing, inquiry, and visualization is the first tool to do a job.

When you go in the business world, you commitment (before making any decision) have a spitting image of the developing process and the outcome of your work.

When such an image takes shape in your mind, you can act more clearly. There has been a lot of debate about visualization, but its status is less debated. Desirable imagery that is based on facts, vision, logic, and rationality will be more realizable than imagery far from reality.

So, visualization as the first basic tool in the business world is of the utmost importance, which should be addressed further.

VISUALIZATION

Giving to Brian Tracy:
"All the successes of your life are possible by improving your mental imagery."

Jim Concert also declares:

"You become the one you see."

In the process of mental imagery, your mind and its visuals must constantly be aware of what you want and the person you want to become. Mental imagery means thinking deeply or concentrating the energy of thought on a particular subject with the image of that subject in mind. Mental imagery is quite similar to external realities.

In addition, mental imagery is acquired and based on creativity, not based on intelligence. Therefore, this method is effective and applicable to all people and all ages. One day a friend said:

- *"Beware of your mental images. Sometimes mental images are plagues."*

Mental imagery is the color and the glaze of the starting point of any job. Do not you think it is better to impregnate your business with nice color and glaze? First, think about the plagues of our imagery.

Mental imagery is now and then a plague to itself. At any time, there is a possibility that your mental images go awry. Deterioration of mental images means turning images into unattainable fantasies. This is an example of a plague. Plagues that can damage our business.

A successful person knows the boundaries and is careful not to fall into the pit of illusion.

The visualization of a successful person will not be distorted and he keeps it strictly under control.

A quote from Albert Einstein:

"Mental imagery is more important than facts."

Let's challenge our minds before a reality occurs and nurture it for a good happening. It is best to keep exercising our minds to welcome good events. This is how we can achieve the best in mental imagery. When a good visualization takes place free of illusions, we can design successful plans to achieve our goals.

Four essential elements for effective mental imagery according to Brian Tracy:

1- Repetition and alternation

The number of times you picture a particular goal in your mind is directly related to reality. The more you repeat that image in your mind, the more it is recorded in your subconscious mind and can easily be part of the reality of your life.

2- Duration

The second element of visualization is its duration. That is, how much time you spend on mental imagery each day.

When you are in a relaxed mood, you can visualize the desired image for a few seconds or even a few minutes. The more you do it, the better you can send the image deep into your subconscious mind.

3 - Clarity and transparency

There is a direct relationship between clear thinking and performance and turning it into reality. When you consider a new goal for yourself, your idea or embodiment of that goal is usually ambiguous. But the more you write, review, and visualize it in your mind, it becomes clearer and more vivid to you and you will eventually find yourself in a situation where the "goal" is fully vivid. At this time, the target suddenly appears in your world, exactly as you pictured it.

4 - Intensity

The intensity of imagery means that we combine our emotions with our imagination. This is the most important part of mental imagery. If your emotions are strong enough and with rich content and your visualization is sufficiently clear, your goal will come true immediately.

PATHWAY DETERMINATION

One of the visualization prerequisites is to determine a path for ourselves that begins at point A and ends at point B. Basically, why should we go when there is no way to go?

Presume you are going to take a trip. What is the prerequisite of this journey that comes to us unconsciously? In fact, the prerequisite for travel is a "road map". This is necessary because we reach our destination easier, faster, and safer. Everyone thinks so. This prerequisite is much more important than the necessities such as travel apparatus.

That is why usually (before a trip) some things are left behind! Because our subconscious mind has been oriented toward the prerequisite, i.e. "to know and determine the path".

Prophet Jesus (PBUH) says:

"There are unknown paths whose travelers are few."

Not everyone can enter every path. Above all those paths that are much unknown. There are many unknown pathways in the business world. Unknown pathways need bold action and a risk-taking attitude. How much of a risk-taker do you consider yourself to be? "Risk" is a requirement of the work, otherwise you will not succeed. History has proved that risks and unknown pathways can lead you to new findings. If there were no risks and unknown routes, then today's amenities would not have had a place in human life.

Frank Clark says:

"If you could find an unobstructed route, you probably will not get anywhere."

If you want to succeed and excel in the business world, you have to embrace risk. Risk, though frightening at times, makes you more mature. A manager must expand the boundaries of his maturity. The boundary of maturity expands as we enter unknown pathways.

Beyond unknown pathways, there are valuable capitals that need to be discovered. Let yourself loose in discovery and exploration, and do not be afraid. On the one hand, a pathway is better to be straight. There is a narrow road between one village and another. The connection between one city with another city is a highway and the connection between a metropolis with another metropolis a superhighway. The more valuable our goals, the straighter a route we must take. It does not matter that the route is long or short or what is the quality of the road. The important thing is the straightforwardness of the path. Enhance the power of moving on the path and exploring the world of pathways in yourself and move on . . .

No cowardly manager succeeds.

No stagnant manager succeeds. No immature entrepreneur is a top-notch entrepreneur.

No genius in the business world strays from unknown paths

WHAT DO WE WANT?

Our lives from *A* to *Z* are tied to "what do we want". If we know what we want in the pathway of our business - we have taken the first step to victory. Earmark this point in your mind:

A journey of a thousand leagues begins with the first step.

Many people have a wish. But they have not made a note. So we conclude that they have no wishes! Having desires requires writing each one of those desires. We have something called a "list".

The "list" sorts out our engagement with our plans.

Successful people get used to writing and having lists. We have to make a comprehensive list of everything in our lives. The wishes we have, the friends we have, the meetings we have, the visits we have and the capitals we have.

Capital is not just cash. This comprehensive list will help us along the way to our goals. When it is clear what we want, let's list them. This will be our most comprehensive asset. A powerful manager must have a complete list of the corporate community and keep reviewing it.

The fact that *'what do we want?'* and *'what is the main priority of our desire?'* will help us through the vicissitudes of our business. It has always been the main theme of the world's greatest and most successful business lecturers that:

"Specify your wish."

Imagine you have entered a store. Upon arrival, the shopkeeper will ask:

- "What do you want?"

It makes no sense that you do not want anything and go into the store without any objective. So you never go into the store without a demand.

In the universe, we are asked the following question every day:

- "What do you want? What do you want from life?"

The one who does not specify his wishes and leaves home certainly does not have a clear logic in life and eventually he will get back into a routine.

More than 90 percent of the world's people do not know what they want and are waiting for their wishes to be set by others. The others prescribe their wishes and those prescriptions mostly benefit the prescriber than the recipients!

How many of these kinds of people do you know around yourself?

Anyone who knows what he wants knows what to do. First, we need to know what we want, to find out the supplies that we need.

If you do not know what you want in life and what your goals are, others will enslave you.

Remember that slaves are not allowed to want anything or

have a purpose.

Dear Manager!

If you do not want your organization to stagnate and fail, bring together your thoughtful and purposeful people and review what your organization wants. What is your organization looking for?

TO MAKE A WISH

Where there is a wish, there is a way. This sentence cannot be easily ignored. Most of the bad things and the good things in every person's life have been at their discretion. So, it turns out that *to want* is a completely internal and powerful element. it could be said:

Other elements do not have the impact of the verb *to want* on the way to achieve the goal.

One day a great speaker (before the lecture began) held up a ten-dollar note and asked the audience:

- "Who wants this ten-dollar bill?"

The crowd shouted in unison:

- "I … I … I …"

The speaker shook his head in regret, then crumpled the ten-dollar bill and shouted a second time:

- "I said who wants this ten-dollar bill?"

Again, the audience shouted:

- "I … I … I …"

The speaker paused a moment and said for the third time

with a loud voice:

- "I ask for a third time. Who wants this ten-dollar bill?"

In the meantime, as the audience were shouting 'I...I...I...', a young boy got out of the crowd and quickly climbed the scene and (like an eagle catching a prey) grabbed the ten-dollar bill from the speaker's hand and fled. The audience started to boo the young boy!

But the speaker said with a laugh:

- "Well done, boy. To want means that... someone who wants something gets up and goes for it. This young boy showed us how to stand up for your desires. To want is different from to like. You just liked the ten-dollar bill. You did not want it. If you wanted it, you would have moved from your place like this young boy..."

Jim Ran says:

"Desires are the prelude to achievements."

The whishes themselves have two categories:

Irrational
Rational

Obviously, no sane person would have an irrational wish. Rational wishes imply paying the cost. You have to pay for every request. The price of fulfilling desires has many types such as "taking the time", "accepting failure" and "losing many things we love". If we find the capacity to take the time, accept the failures, and lose, surely our "wants" will become our "capacities". If there are no such models, then all students who now have their own goals and dreams of success will become doctors or engineers.

In a classroom, there are one, two to three gifted students who are eager to achieve great goals. Not everyone is alike.

You have also people in your organization who have paid for achieving their demands. They have suffered damages. They are powerful people. Find them and take advantage of what they know.

Individuals who have fought for and paid for their desires are valuable assets of an organization, not decadent human resources.

It is mainly because of the fear of failures and the time and loss that many of the wishes will not be fulfilled.

How many of these types of people do you see around you? The same people who have given up every action for fear of failure.

Let us not forget that every wish has a price.

LIST OF GOALS

A list of goals clears up our relationship with our plans. Successful people get used to writing and having a list of goals. You need to list everything in your life.

Your wishes, your friends, your meetings, your capitals, and this comprehensive list will help you achieve your goals.

Many of the outcasts in the community are frustrated when faced with their list of wishes and goals.

They are so troubled in the confusion that they will eventually have to succumb to the disgusting and bad economic and livelihood conditions. This is not what humanity deserves.

A set of building materials such as cement, plaster, brick, iron beams and rods and other things together can construct a building. If it is not a comprehensive list, one cannot expect to build the building. Having a comprehensive and clear list is essential in constructing and achieving the goal.

Now, what does this list contain? You know better. It is important to have a comprehensive list. A strong manager must have a comprehensive and robust organizational list.

At one of the specialized meetings of a chemical materials

and products company, which I was present as a guest, the vice president of the company quoting from the CEO, explained the list of company goals on the whiteboard to the senior managers. In that list, what caught my attention the most was the schedule set to meet each of the goals.

For example, their to-do list indicated that from the third day of the current month to the eighth day of the next third month the status quo must be preserved. The schedule showed that from a certain day to another day, the deputy of development and commerce should do market research. In another place, they indicated, from a certain day to another day, research into competitors' products and market pull. The other section stated . . . from this day to the other day, three experts must examine the customer needs. At another place, it stated . . . from this day to that day, consider the new idea of the female consultant . . .

By looking at such a table, one good point comes to mind, i.e. the company's trajectory for achieving goals is clear. All influential elements and factors of the company must go as planned and the tasks are based on the "get" and "do" cycle. This is a valuable benchmark in the organizational system that a successful manager can have as a "list of goals" about his plans.

FINANCIAL GOALS

Money is an excuse for many of our efforts. Money is not a bad thing; love it so it will be attracted to you. For those who believe money is of no value, the money will escape them and they will always be poor. Goals that have financial implications require further efforts. Do you know why?

Because making money is the art of trading.

Because it is hard to make money.

Because making money requires ingenuity and creativity.

Because making money requires a strong will and a serious decision.

Because making money requires wit and curiosity.

If it were easy to make money, all the people in the world would be rich.

Wealth will be valuable when it comes to toil. Once you are ready to deal with the problems, you deserve to get rich. It is a fact. Bill Gates (one of the richest men in the world) said somewhere:

- "Everybody wants to be in my place. But none are willing to experience the hardships I have endured."

In the business world, financial goals are a precursor to other goals. Because of money matters. Because money can work. Because money opens doors. Because money is first and foremost, a progressive and not a deterrent element.

When it comes to financial goals, what stands out is that there is a big difference between a normal life and a great life.

"Financial goals" guarantee the survival of an organization.

Money and financial capital are the basis of a business. Share your financial goals with the best financial advisors who are very motivated in getting rich. Financial advisers tie your smallest matters with money. The strategy of top advisers is to create both financial attractions and a platform for getting rich. But why we talk about consultants?

Since spending and making money in a profitable business requires expertise and skill, consulting and using the advice of investment experts seems necessary. In this regard, the best advisers are those who have made a profit. One who has no successful experience in the field should not be consulted.

BUSINESS GOALS

Business goals are a set of goals in which your limits and powers are more defined. Your work is categorized in its format and the *A* to *Z* of the path is specified. The business goals include a comprehensive list of where to start and where to reach.

The boundaries and powers you have defined for yourself are very effective. You will be looking for your organizational goals rather than individual and partial goals. But remember, your work goals grow only when you are on the path to growth and excellence.

The stagnation of your mind is equal to the stagnation of your organizational structure. Therefore, in discussing business goals, one must always move forward. Managers who are involved in achieving their own and their organization's business goals have always outstripped their work teams. They are always ahead and always up to date. With an outdated and backward approach, it is not possible to move the business goals on the track of success.

Your business goals come about when you add things to

them. Like an idea. Like new attitudes and like product diversity. Alternatively, like finding talents in the bulk of the organization and from the heart of the human resources.

Steve Jobs had said somewhere:

- *"The reason I formed a powerful organization comes from the fact that I wanted to run my organization in the future."*

Proper attitude, foresight, and vision can also be key elements in achieving your business goals. Your work goals are in the spotlight.

People and customers are always scrutinizing your organization and company at all times.

They want to figure out what you do and see the pure changes you have made to achieve your business goals.

Your business goals (whether you like it or not) will eventually be revealed with the changes that appear in all areas, including product change, work efficiency and procedural change, and even the unveiling of ideas. Therefore, your business goals should be goals that lead to attraction, boosting customer base and excellence in the organization. Business goals occur when you have to get out of stagnation. So, the customer will not be disappointed with you.

Stagnation equals organizational death.

Do you think the stagnant marshland and the flowing river are no different?

When your business goals begin to flow, you are on the path to construction and excellence. Your business goals should not stay on the first step. The next steps await your action. In order to accomplish your business goals, focus on embracing change. Be competitive and be idealistic. Your products must be diverse, and ultimately, your customer service should be responsive.

When an organization or a large company has no business goals, it becomes bankrupt and deteriorates. For example, when it does not embrace change and when it has fixed geography. There are other factors that you know better.

Do not assign specific geography to your business goals. Let your business goals be out of bounds. If you are still and immobile and stay the same, you will become repetitive and old. If you do not make the right changes to meet your business goals, customers will lose confidence in you.

Finally, I suggest that you use the most skilled people in the organization to write and formulate the best business goals for your organization. They have new ideas and attitudes that you have probably never heard of before. Do not attempt all by yourself. A good quote from Brian Tracy:

"Your income is influenced by three factors: . . .

- What you do.

- You do it well.

- Replacing you will be difficult."

Jim Ran also says:

- *"My father has taught me to always work more for the salary I earn to make it capital for my future."*

GOALS AND OTHERS

How effective are other people's goals in growing and flourishing your goals? Identify it for yourself and think about it well. Not all of the people around us are wily and crafty. This micro-goals of others can complement your higher goals.

Sometimes it is the goals of others that boost our vision on the path to our goals.

By others, we mean close friends, relatives, staff and competitors. We have a solution for you: ask your staff to design a trajectory for your organization. What is wrong with that?

Talk to trustworthy people about your goals.

Unless you talk with others, others won't talk about their plans or suggestions.

"Market rewards best goals."

Get help from elite staff who have ideas, pristine plans, and growth-trigger programs. Do not lock yourself in a private room and think you know everything!

Certainly, you have capable people with ideas in your

organization.

Just do some research and find them. More than seventy percent of the goals you are pursuing are thought by seventy percent of people in the community! If you want to achieve at least one of those goals, take the ideas of one percent of that seventy percent seriously.

I promise you will not lose it. So, others can change a significant part of our lives if we give them a chance. Brian Tracy has written in one of his books:

"An important part of goal setting is to identify the individuals, groups, and organizations that will help you achieve your goals. Identify capable people related to your business. Ask your staff to come up with ideas. Reward their ideas and encourage them to focus their minds on helping the organization grow. It is alright."

Do not get falsely arrogant in the business, because you will fall.

Others can be effective in making your goals clear. Others can complement us, give advice and formulate solutions . . . There are capitals in the chain of others that need to be discovered. A winning manager devotes part of his daily job to do the following:

- "Which of the staff under his command has a solution? Which of the staff under his command has the right solution?"

Others are not always going to be blindly at your service. They also have insights.

Discovering valuable human resources inventory is one of the key tasks of a successful manager.

Make a list of effective, thoughtful, and ingenious individuals among the people you have. Review this list every day and work on a topic you need to do using effective staff to create a work team, and the last but not least is that others know things that probably we may not know.

Some of these others may not be wiser than us, but certainly, most of the other people are wiser than us.

ELEMENT OF COMMITMENT

You do not have to make a promise to anyone to accomplish your goals at all. This is a hidden pit in the business world.

We want to address the issue of "others" from another angle. Admittedly, while others are good at helping us to achieve our goals, the reality is that others are pursuing their goals before they even think about their goals. Therefore, commitment to others has no meaning other than dependence on them. If it is for others that you consider yourself committed to doing things, you are very wrong. Under these circumstances, you will not see the dawn of success. The interpretation of true commitment goes far beyond that.

Real commitment means being committed to yourself. That is to say, promise yourself to accept responsibility.

To change the situation, a strong and firm promise is needed.

So you must and must and must commit to yourself and stay committed. If you are a committed person, I promise you no negative wavelength and no failing attitudes will prevail over you.

The rulers consider themselves committed.

The rulers commit themselves to carry out matters. They free themselves from dependence, although they do not disagree with the advice and assistance of others.

Dear Manager!

Everything starts with you and continues with you.

One day a journalist asked a wealthy artisan:

- "What if you lose all your wealth?"

The craftsman laughed and said:

- "I start again and with creativity, perseverance, and commitment, I get the wealth that I have now."

A successful manager must be committed to achieving his own goals before being committed to achieving the goals of others. Empower yourself as much as possible in having a covenant with yourself. Be sure, if there is no commitment, nothing will move on. A simple office worker who arrives early morning and punches his card in the time clock gives the most interesting type of commitment!

This employee knows well that he should expect dismissal if he does not arrive on time. So, timely arrival and commitment to a constant presence in the workplace are one of the most important elements of his working life. But in fact, this kind of commitment is not a commitment made by the great and successful people of society and the self-made wealthy ones. This commitment is an obligation based on dutifulness in work with the hope of receiving simple government salaries. The type of commitment in the successful management structure and work structure of progressive individuals is the one in which there is always growth and excellence and the growth is felt. What kind of personal growth and excellence are there in the field of staffing that we need to address or brag about? Except for the entrusted positions that should sooner or later be handed over to the next people!

So with these interpretations, you (as a progressive manager) should consider your situation from today to the next three to five years. You are one of the most successful and profitable people in your field of business. What needs to happen to get to that position? Find it and commit to it. This is a working model. Write it down somewhere.

This is you who decide how to commit to yourself.

What does one expect of the staff when a manager is not committed to himself or his organization?

This is the obvious reason for many problems in organizations, agencies, and corporations. "Refusing commitment". The first step in commitment is to keep your word. In the eyes of the people, your personality is measured by your commitments. Your organization has a personality and a value for itself too. Do not play with it.

The whole value of an organization's personality depends on its commitments.

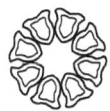

LET'S BE COMMITTED

When asked about the secret to the success of successful corporate executives, usually their answer is: we were committed to our commitments.

As you are reading this book, you have been under a great deal of pressure for many commitments. Right?

Roll up your sleeve and list your commitments immediately. Perhaps many of them have been forgotten.

Underestimating commitments are playing with an organization's survival.

Be very careful. The organization can be easily destroyed but not easily built. Remember, you need two characteristics to win "to get committed" and "to carry out the commitment".

A side note:

Not every responsible person is committed. Nevertheless, any committed person can be responsible.

Committed people are always offered good suggestions. Never forget this. A commitment-oriented responsibility will always be a forward-looking responsibility and will drive incremental growth in the organization.

Dear Manager!

Get yourself accustomed to accepting responsibilities you are capable of and can do. Otherwise, stop working before losing your job. There is nothing worse for a manager than losing his credibility and reliability. It is much more difficult to accept responsibility than to conquer Everest! Keep in mind, too, that accepting too many responsibilities is not just about being responsible, it is just about being busy! There are a lot of people in the community as directors who are very occupied, and despite their many positions and jobs, their work output is zero!

But on the other hand, everything a great and successful manager does has a good output. No efficient manager is empty-handed and stays empty-handed. He has always many reserves. Being a very occupied manager both diminishes the quality of output and brings the quality of responsibility into question. In general, such a manager is burdened with commitments, some of which may be his most critical organizational covenants, and the breach of the promise and the breach of the commitment will cause a fatal blow to his establishment.

Which very busy person do you know who is committed? So many small things surround him that he fails to fulfill his small or big commitments! To put it simply: "No *drive-by* manager can be found behind his desk."

The multi-position and invisible manager loses his buyers. This is an undeniable principle in the management system. It is usually proven that people tend to be more attracted to accessible managers than to managers who are lost! So, the conclusion is that: either do not accept heavy responsibilities or if you do, consult committed and knowledgeable people who can ease some of your work and seek their help.

Ali (AS) says in *Nahj al-Balagha*:

- *"There is no support and backing like a consultation."*

Consultation is a source of guidance. Consultation brings you the right ideas of others. So, work harder on commitments such as "commitment to yourself"; "commitment to your subordinate colleagues and personnel" and "commitment to customers" and go ahead carefully. If you are committed to heavy responsibilities, remember that properly performing heavy duties in an organization requires three important factors:

- *Consultation with elites and related specialists (consultation)*

- *Accurate anatomy of accountability accepted (research)*

- *Creating an executive and committed working group (teamwork)*

An interesting point to note is that the personnel and forces under your command (based on their duties and habits) consider themselves obligated to do things. They consider themselves committed. So, take the best advantage of their presence to make things better.

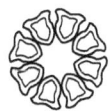

COMMITMENT, CONSISTENCY OF PERSONALITY

The first step of commitment is to make sure you will be true to your word. When someone has double-talk, it is clear that he cannot be trusted.

In all our social interactions and action-reaction in our lives, there is commitment and it is felt. The same little components that have acquired the color and glaze of commitment in our lives can also influence our personality development and strengthen us in undertaking commitment. So they should not be easily overlooked.

If we feel powerless to promise to ourselves, we must have had a past full of non-commitment.

The skewed trunk of a tree dates back to its seedling period. An untrustworthy person who loses his popularity in the community will no doubt be an unsuccessful person in his business commitments. Clearly, part of a manager's personality in the social field depends on the amount of his commitment and the performance of his obligations. It happens before the community goes on to focus on a manager's revenue, expertise, and profession.

As a manager, you are (willingly or unwillingly) obligated to many of your customers and people. Be careful not to get caught up in the pit of non-commitment since your personality will be completely in question.

A majority of the growth of an organization depends on the manager's personality.

Damage to the manager's personality is also equivalent to damage to organizational structure. Such damage can destroy even a large corporation.

Remember that besides you, dear manager, all of your organizational and staffing factors have personality and have a value for themselves. These personalities and values should not be played with.

In the management field, personality depends on commitment and commitment to personality.

The non-committed manager strikes the first blow to himself. Given the importance of commitment, be sure to work on it and strengthen your commitment.

The result is that underestimating commitments is playing with the position of the organization, and this is extremely dangerous. Be careful.

In order to be a good and trusted brand, you need to be true to your commitments and keep your commitments to the fullest extent possible. Customers want that.

COMMITMENT IN LINE WITH THE RESPONSIBILITY

When it comes to big business, the matters will be a bit complicated. Much more complicated than you might think. That is no reason for a manager to step back and escape from the challenge. This is not a reason for a manager not to be burdened with heavy obligations. Basically, "management" means facing challenges, failures and starting over.

Dr. Johnson says:

- *"There are always valleys between the peaks. The decisive factor to reach the next peak sooner or later is how to manage their valley."*

You have obviously begun to grow and excel and accept big jobs, otherwise, you would not go into management. Therefore, from this day you have to develop yourself to do great things. Do not try to be satisfied with the status quo. Otherwise, forget about growth and do not undertake any responsibility. It is with your growth that your organization grows.

Excellent goals await powerful and self-assured executives

with great commitment and responsibility. An inefficient and weak manager cannot handle heavy responsibilities. You are well aware of what to do if you do not evade responsibility.

Clearly, the bigger your organization is, the bigger its management will be and it needs a huge management structure. Its management must also be subject to high obligations and responsibilities. This is a very difficult operation.

Woe to the day when a dysfunctional manager comes to the fore. The catastrophe that results from such appointments will be very destructive and devastating. It is like giving a -10year-old kid a Lamborghini car's switch and put him behind the wheel. You know better what an awful end awaits the awkward driver and the car itself.

You have certainly seen and heard a lot of news about the adjustments, layoffs, riots, workers' strikes and bankruptcies of big companies and organizations in the media. These events are partly related to the problematic policies of governments and much of it to the same awkward management mentioned in the Lamborghini switch and the child example.

The foremost cause of bankruptcy and corporate destruction is poor and weak management.

An example:

How a child walks in his father's loose shoes? Can he walk at all? This baby will keep falling (although daddy's shoes are of the best type).

The wisest way is to size the shoes to fit the child's growth.

Dear manager!

If you want big responsibilities to accomplish your goals, try small responsibilities first to get ready. The same tests will determine your grade. The ups and downs of business and trade are experienced in light of these small responsibilities. Such experiences are valuable assets that are essential to train a manager. Do not be afraid of the obstacles on the way of big responsibilities because such fear will destroy you. There is no river that has not endured the experience of dealing with rocks and sands.

I read somewhere:

- "The pleasant song of the river is the result of a collision with rocks."

The last word:

Great commitments and responsibilities are frightening but can be overpowered.

In fact, the more you have mastered your big responsibilities, your price will go higher and higher.

The higher your price, the more expensive your organization will be. Many an organization and company is willing to spend millions of dollars to attract powerful, responsible executives. Where are you in this equation?

ACCOUNTABILITY

Accountable people only realize true commitment. An accountable person is definitely a committed person. So, the relationship between commitment and responsibility is a close one. Not every responsible person is committed, but every committed person can be accountable.

- "Commitment is one step before accountability."

Accountability is tied to a key point, which is the "can do" attitude. Get yourself accustomed to accepting the responsibilities you are capable of and can do. It is natural that any person neither knows everything nor is capable of anything. Therefore, in these circumstances, obligations cannot be fulfilled without taking into account individual and environmental conditions. Especially in the difficult field of management.

People are empowered by the experiences they gain in their favorite profession. So, it seems a bit of good advice when we say you should accept responsibility for work depending on your ability. Accepting too many responsibilities does not imply accountability.

Unless you succeed in researching the situation, you should not bear any responsibility since it will cost you dearly. Customers and buyers always expect managers to do things. Managers who are weak are deceived by the volume of expectations and fall short of their obligations and responsibilities, but prudent managers weigh all expectations against their own circumstances and then commit to them.

Customers' expectations result in a huge responsibility.

Sit down and listen to the bankrupt and isolated executives who have lost their business and economic dynasty to understand what the consequences of inadequate acceptation of responsibility are.

We highlight these things to you and would love to give you a cure before the accident. You must try to review your commitments and responsibilities, and do not accept anything and do not fall prey to it.

Your responsibilities determine the boundaries and scope of your activities.

It is not genius to have a huge scope of work authority and brag about it. The genius is to properly organize and manage such boundaries in the scope of responsibility. The kings that have conquered vast countries throughout history and increased their powers and authorities have soon lost their grip of government; except for the kings who were very powerful in their rule.

Do not get your management system entrapped in the line of responsibilities that will disturb you, to be able to move forward conveniently.

DIVISION OF RESPONSIBILITY

As the responsibilities are shared in a small family and everyone is familiar with his/her job, you need to see your organization from this perspective. An organization may also be disrupted in the field of the division of responsibilities. Remember, no one in an unstable and disorderly army will obey another person.

Everybody plays his own instrument, which is a disaster and such an organization must be shut down! When there is no accurate knowledge of staff capability, when relatives and acquaintances have a strong preference over capable personnel, do not doubt that such an organization will go nowhere.

With the right division of responsibility in the organization, you can achieve your goals more easily.

You may have heard this a couple of times:

- "In that system, no one is in their place! Matters become very hard when no one is in their place."

The organization's engine will fail. Be very careful about the division of responsibility and its importance. Think of the puzzle pieces. Each piece of the puzzle has an important role in itself. These pieces must be definitely in place. Because they are defined for a specific vacant space.

Successful managers take into account the talent and potential of their staff before they care about ethnicity and tribal relationships. That is, who has what abilities, which person is good for what department?

The talented personnel used in their own right are aces up the sleeve of a manager. Often, there are several principles prevailing the proper division of responsibility:

- Staff satisfaction

- Work expedition

- Management's luck

Remember James McTillow's advice:

- "While you need to be serious with people to avoid reverse assignments, take heed of their struggling. Teaching and support is part of a manager's job."

There is a psychological principle that says: ... neither a child can assume the real responsibility of the father, nor a mother. Neither the father has the power to accept the real responsibility of the mother, nor the child. More importantly, parents were once small children in their families and experienced many obstacles and difficulties up to the stage of assuming responsibility.

In an organization (such as a family), everyone should be assigned to work in defined positions and responsibilities based on maturity, experience, and expertise. I stress it again.

Think about the puzzle while dividing the responsibilities.

It is important to know those very close friends and relatives employed in the organization rarely go under the burden of commitment and responsibility. Experience in this regard has shown that a greater percentage of cliques in the organization have been associated with frustration and failure in the field of "division of responsibility and assignment of positions to relatives". You do not want to be on the list of frustrated people, right? So, delegate the tasks to the qualified people. Give responsibility to competent persons with high performance and operational capability. Properly handing over of the matters by the manager, gives him a wider field of action to move things forward. James McTillow says in the book *Time Management*:

- "Outsourcing tasks by the manager frees him to focus on the tasks that are most in need of his attention."

John C. Maxwell also says:

- "Find and develop the scope of capabilities of your subordinates to become a strong manager."

Moreover, I read elsewhere:

- "There are always valleys between the peaks. The decisive factor to reach the next peak sooner or later is how to manage their valley."

General Patton says:

- "Never tell people how to get things done. Tell them what to do. They will surprise you with their skills."

BIG RESPONSIBILITIES

From today, try to develop yourself to manage big matters. But what are the big matters? In simple and empirical terms, macro matters are the scope of activities that (while branching into clusters) encompass several micro matters. When your business is on the path to growth and excellence, your micro matters are shifted to the macro matters and your business system expands.

Have you prepared yourself for such a day? You may not have taken the matter seriously, arguing that years of experience (for managing big matters) will help you, but I must say that years of experience are not enough.

Let's identify the factors that will help you manage macro matters and develop yourself by doing them correctly. Do not wait for the big things to come to you. The macro matters are so complex and layered that they will destroy you if you are not ready. Most of the time, big matters are like devastating seasonal hurricanes. Be careful about this. Every manager who seeks to grow and excel in his organization anticipates facing big issues and adds to his knowledge and ability every day. Because facing big issues requires not only experience but also the right thought and expertise.

In task assignment, we must be careful that everything flows in our organizational system through small and large clusters. Some small tasks can easily be left to those from whom you do not expect too much. Some big tasks can also be given to capable people who have both great talent and expertise. Therefore, apart from the rule of division of responsibility, it is important to know the micro and the macro matters. Now, let's focus on macro matters.

Not everyone can do great things. Great jobs need great people. In the organizational and administrative system, there are matters called "macro matters" due to high dispersion and volume. Be very careful in accepting macro matters. Macro matters - as the title shows - entail huge burden.

Those who engage in big issues think big, plan big and manage big. From this day, separate the macro matter elements from micro matter elements to become gradually prepared.

Try not to be content with the day-to-day routine while preparing for macro-management. Those who are satisfied with their day-to-day conditions must forget about growth, excellence, and acceptance of responsibility, right now. You need to be sophisticated enough in doing micro matters to further (at some point) change them into macro matters and start managing them.

For a manager, the best thing is to test macro matters. Macro matters also require great insight and knowledge. Macro matters, though they have their own twist, turns, and (like a complex maze) seem confusing, but these complexities and metabolisms will bring about the maturity of the manager.

Big things will come to you willy-nilly. Do not shy

away from them. When your organization is in the growth stage, do not doubt that your work and responsibilities will experience an expanding and large-scale process.

Big matters need their own big vision.

So, you cannot imagine that there will be no big matters anymore. Sooner or later big matters will come to you. Just keep yourself ready for such an event; lest big matters tie up your hands and legs when you do not know what to do! And what team should be recruited to solve problems!

Being caught like that will be to your loss. When you are involved in big things, you need to think big and plan big. Having a pickup van, you cannot be hired at a large transit transportation company to carry their cargo to and from the cities. A transit transportation company requires a trailer truck.

Task-oriented managers cannot manage big matters.

For a senior manager, the small responsibilities ahead are not a big deal. Does an eighteen-wheeler trailer truck feel the grit on the road pavement? Basically, the grit is not an obstacle for a truck with eighteen wheels. The macro manager also has such a characteristic.

A macro manager is not afraid of obstacles.

He knows well that there are obstacles always and everywhere. He has also accepted that something that is always visible is not scary. By daily engagement in micro matters, train yourself to eventually undertake big matters. Remember those big responsibilities have the advantage of increasing your price.

According to one of the thinkers:

- *"Do the great and important things yourself and leave the small things to others."*

Isaac Newton says:

- *"If I have seen further, it is by standing on the shoulders of Giants."*

From today, separate your micro matters from macro matters and devise a plan for it. Find the defect in your managerial practice to do such big matters correctly. Fix that defect.

BODY AND REASON

Somewhere I read:
- *"Some people have minds ahead of their bodies and some people have their bodies ahead of their mind."*

The meaning of the above sentence is very clear. Many people live up to 25 and are buried at 90! These people have spent 65 years of their precious lives in their daily routines (like a moving object), but their minds are sealed and most of the time they are complaining about others and why they have such a miserable life! There is no growth and trouble follows trouble! Misery after misery.

They always expect others to do something for them! Administrations to come, relatives with good connections, or friends having great responsibilities! Take a look at their lives. Do you see anything but whimpering and complaining? More than 80 percent of the world's population lives the same way. But a person should not live like that.

God Almighty has bestowed the gift of the mind only to a being such as a human as the highest of the creatures and has not given it to any other creature. With such a worthy gift in human beings, it is unfortunate for him to live a dirty life.

The human mind has two aspects: first, the information it can store and second, what it can do.

Mind and thought are created to provide us with a good life. It was the power of the progressive human mind that led him from the Stone Age to the agricultural age, and from the agricultural age to the industrial age, and subsequently to the age of technology, otherwise, our body looks like the body of primitive humans.

Let me tell you an interesting fact: If you stretch your arm, you occupy something about 2 feet of space while your mind can conquer the world.

The mind of successful managers is always ahead of their body. This is a prerequisite for success. Your organization desperately needs your strong mind rather than your body. You have to think, think and think again.

Define a think tank for your management department and strive to develop your thoughts. Closing down your mind should never happen. This closure is the shutdown of the foundation of your business. When you are in the field of management, be very careful about mental stagnation.

Your mind needs food for ideas and creativity. Including study, communication, gaining experience and so on. All of these factors lead you to victory. Do not worry about filling up your mind! Your mind is a huge repository that holds a lot of data. In fact, what is endless is science and knowledge.

The manager of one of the largest manufacturing companies is a physically disabled person. It is interesting to know that the executives and personnel of this production company are also physically disabled, i.e. blind, deaf, mute and paralyzed!

The company slogan is also installed on the company façade.

We need thoughts, not individuals.

What if, for example, one day instead of working, the staff gather in the think tank room and comment on the matters? Introduce their ideas and present a thesis. Write a plan for the organization and give a solution. Remember that we humans all have the power of analysis. Whether a simple worker or an office clerk.

THE RICH MIND

One day, Einstein's friend came to visit the great scientist. After a long discussion, Einstein's friend said at the exit:

- *"Tell me your home phone number to put it down."*

Einstein pointed to the desk drawer and said:

- *"The home phone number is in the phonebook in the drawer. Go pick up the phone book and write!"*

Einstein's friend asked in surprise:

- *"You mean you do not even remember your home phone number?"*

Einstein replied:

- *"My mind is not about storing a handful of nonsensical numbers. There are more important things to store in it!"*

Remembering a thousand phone numbers is not a genius. The genius is keeping a whole bunch of growth ideas and attitudes in our minds. This is how it becomes a rich mind.

There is no self-made and successful man who has not taken advantage of his powerful mind. The rich mind can make you rich. The rich mind is capable of making you a very powerful person possessing creativity and attitude. The actions and reactions of man throughout his life, his successes and failures, his growth and stagnation and all other things depend on the strength and weakness of his mind.

If you believe in the rich mind you will become rich. If you do not believe, you will not get anywhere.

In this universe, nothing is as valuable as a healthy mind.

John Edder had said somewhere:

- "If you do not work out your brain throughout life and do not keep it active, this lethargy will increase. Therefore, use your brain. Otherwise, you will lose it."

A rich mind is a mind that is active, creative, idealistic and clear.

A rich mind is a mind that is refined and has progressive thoughts. It is constantly gaining experience and information and is aiming for growth and excellence.

An anecdote:

... One day a student of Einstein was passing by a park. In the middle of the path, he saw a little girl throwing rocks into the pond in the middle of the park! He immediately went to the little girl and asked her why. The little girl said playfully:

- "When I throw a stone into the water, there are circular waves. I want to throw the stone such that the waves are square!"

Einstein's student, himself an experienced physicist, laughed by the little girl's reply. A few minutes later, he explained to the girl on a piece of paper that based on such and such equations of physics, that would not be possible and her effort is in vain! Seeing the complicated equations on the paper, the little girl was convinced and left. Einstein's student went on his way after the explanation. Einstein asked the reason for the delay as soon as he saw the student, and the student told him about the girl. It was here that Einstein yelled at the student:

- "What a big mistake! How dared you stop the little girl's efforts with a few simple and complicated equations? We know it is impossible, but what if it could be done! Maybe this little girl could have made a great discovery! Perhaps with her findings, the world would change a lot!"

If we understand the capabilities of our rich minds, use them, and know what a valuable treasure we have at our disposal, we are on the path to prosperity. The rich mind seeks change, development, and growth. Catherine Pander has written somewhere:

- "A rich mind is more powerful than a thousand defeat-seeking minds, and two rich minds stronger than 10,000 weak and defeat-seeking minds."

Avoid submitting the control of your rich mind to others.

The most humiliating form of life is that our rich minds are enslaved to others. If others are to determine the limits and powers of your mind, you will remain an absolutely failed person. In the book *The Law of Might* we read:

"... the only crown that others put on your head is to tear apart the beautiful images you made for your own life with their skepticism and mistrust."

Joseph Murphy also says:

- *"Look at your mind as a garden. You are the gardener..."*

You should always have an empty bowl to get valuable information.

Not everyone believes in an empty bowl. Many have a full bowl of mind. They know things up to a point and have no more vacancy. In fact, they do not really want to put something in their minds anymore! If at some point we say use the minds of others to move things forward, it is because not everybody thinks similarly.

Among people, there are people whose minds are ahead of their bodies.

And lastly, a phrase from Jim Ran:

- *"Do not use your mind as a file cabinet, use it to analyze problems and find solutions."*

THE GRAVITY OF THE MIND

One of the realities of the world around us is the gravitational power of the Earth, and one of the wonders of human existence is the gravitational power of the mind. That is why they say 'life is the sum total of our thoughts'. Our mind has the power to create the life we love and it depends on our take of it.

A ring consists of two parts: shank and center stone.

The human body is the shank and his mind is the center stone.

Just as we see a ring, we focus on its center stone, when we meet people in the community, their thoughts, and mental perceptions become more apparent to us than anything else does. How much do you think a ring without center stone is worth?

Unfortunately, most people say:

- "I cannot do more than this! I have to be realistic. I have to be satisfied with the status quo and accept my fate."

This is the most cowardly type of thinking. The mind in the center of human existence attracts many people. This type of attraction is the first gravitational power of the mind.

Basically, people are attracted to those who know more. People who have progressive wisdom and thoughts. You are an irresistible magnet that can attract big dreams and the right demands. Your mind is so powerful that it can attract hundreds of millions of people. If you do not believe it, read Mahatma Gandhi's biography. We all know that people have an attraction or repulsion power based on their minds and beliefs.

Successful executives have more attraction than repulsion. The best quality an attractive manager can have is that those around him constantly learn something through his behavior, speech, thoughts, plans, actions, and reactions. Let's not forget that the most important factor in attracting people is "knowledge" and "awareness".

In your opinion, is there any wise and mature human being following the path of an ignorant one?

The powerful mind is a knowledgeable mind, and knowledge and awareness flow throughout it. If you want to influence society and have an attitude and style, you need to look at your mental attractions. The quality of your existence depends on the charm of your mind and your real price is evaluated based on these qualities.

An expensive manager has expensive clients.

Why did Nissan Co. (when it was on the verge of bankruptcy) recruit Carlos Gossen and put him in a position of management? Because Gossen had driven the growth of another rival carmaker firm. He was an expensive manager. As a manager having plans, you desperately need mental and business support. Otherwise, you will lose many of the effective people in your organization.

Napoleon Hill says:

- "A successful manager must change his or her mental hue (like a chameleon) to accommodate any challenge in management. Without this ability, no manager can stay strong and continue on the path to growth."

POWER OF THOUGHT

As a manager, you need to know that no other mechanism works for your organization more than "thinking"
We all live in a world of thoughts and ideas.
Thinking can lead to valuable findings.
By thinking, you can come up with a variety of solutions (which will pave the way through rough terrain).
A manager must be able to think well and pay attention to good thoughts.
Basically, the organization without thinking will be a hollowed-out organization. When something breaks, the reason is a hollowness. Dynamic thinking reinforces the foundation for an organization and prevents organizational breakdowns.
A manager must be able to think and present it.
A manager must think and constantly think and think constantly.
Look for thoughts, not individuals.
You see every type of people around you. But there are no

good thoughts! Good thoughts are less than the number of people. So, finding good thoughts is also a necessity in itself.

Identify and visit the thoughtful people in your organization. Listen to them and implement their plans as much as possible. Remember, your real assets are the people with the right ideas and thoughts, not your industrial buildings and machines and bank accounts.

Tomorrow, tomorrow, and tomorrows, there will be shops on the streets that sell thoughts instead of selling goods! How much do you believe in this? I suggest you focus on this important matter.

At present, the owners of ideas and thoughts are being priced.

From now on, identify the thoughtful people who pace around you with ideas. They will lead you to the summit of success. Rest assured.

John Edder says:

- *"Someone who wants to solve problems effectively, must think and ask good questions from himself and others. Questions are wrenches that unscrew the mind."*

Jim Ran also mentioned somewhere:

- *"Nothing is more powerful than gathering good ideas, thoughts, and information. Do this as your daily homework."*

If you have to skip a meal to have a chat with thoughtful people, go ahead.

By constantly thinking about fear, worry, anger, hatred, and failure, you will become depressed. Remember, your life is made of the same thoughts that are inside you. What is certain is secret to the success of all great executives is "to know" and "to do".

An example of an Italian manager's thinking power:

    ...This Italian manager owned a large store that was robbed three times! But instead of complaining about the theft, the thoughtful manager ordered a billboard to be installed at the store's entrance, saying: "Dear fellow citizens, as you have been informed, this store has been robbed thrice! Do you see better proof of the quality of our goods?

UNDERSTANDING THE WORK

Understanding an action is much more important than being capable of doing it.

A manager who does not take the time to learn all the details of his job is doomed to failure.

One of the causes of business failure is a lack of understanding of the job. Many managers work by the routine and enjoy natural growth, but in fact, they do not really understand the work!

One way to correctly understand the work is to know the most detailed work patterns. These partial matters make up the whole. Organizational understanding and cognition is the best driver of the management strategy.

A question as an example:

In your opinion, for a ship captain, what is the first thing he has to know ... (think for a moment).

The answer is definitely *swimming*.

A ship captain must dominate the most important part of the seafaring that is "swimming ability". Not swimming in the pool but swimming in deep waters!

Why might one who is unfamiliar with the swimming techniques hold the wheel of a ship?

A school principal must have experienced the student years himself. He must first be a teacher to be able to sit on the management chair. He must have a good understanding of the education system. Do you know a mechanic who does not know how to drive? On the other hand, a chef who does not distinguish good rice from poor rice?

In the field of management, only when you master the details of a job, you will be able to do it well.

ABOUT DELL INC.

The CEO of Dell Inc. first involved himself in the manufacture and repair of computer equipment before deciding to manufacture personal computers. Michael Dell discovered his passion for computers at the age of 15.

When his parents gifted him an Apple computer, Michael disassembled it completely instead of using it to understand how a computer works by investigating the parts. Then he bought an IBM computer and began to identify its components and how to assemble a computer. He eventually mastered the know-how, which helped him become a billionaire at a young age.

As much as you understand your work, you have helped your organization grow.

Bill Gates, the owner of Microsoft Corporation, had engaged himself in the most elaborate of computer technical matters. This involvement and endurance of work hardships were one of his characteristics from a young age (with his mindset on making a global breakthrough in the computer industry). Bill Gates is without a doubt the most capable manager the world has ever seen. A high-profile manager told me at a conference:

- "A good understanding of work is equal to a good defense of work."

It is better for the head of a sports federation to have already (more or less) tried his hand in that sport, otherwise, he will not understand what the athletes in that field demand.

I knew a manager who was known as a drive-by manager! The manager who arrived signed and went away! What does one expect from such a manager? Will one expect him to build a successful organization?

The only way out of work problems is to understand the work. You have to get involved with work. The best fertilizer for the farm is the farmer's footprint.

The more you understand your work, the more you have helped your organization grow. A manager who keeps himself away from the challenges and ups and downs and is reluctant to face the ebb and flow with a low performance will get into trouble.

The staff is mindful of the manager. They will never fail in their assigned tasks when they realize the manager's grasp and understanding of matters. Do you think a student who does not understand the lesson scores well or a student who understands that lesson? The more you understand the work, the better you will be able to defend it. Although you are a manager, you are actually a student in the business world.

Without ever realizing yourself, you are constantly receiving workplace experiences and interactions with your business. So, it is best to have a good understanding of business lessons in order to get a high score for success and growth, and do not skip it until you get the details.

GOOD FEELING

When you love yourself and believe that few people are like you and that you have valuable elements, you have actually tied your insides to good feelings. This can be a valuable factor in personality development.

You deserve the best.

The first priority in your life is yourself. John C. Maxwell has written somewhere:

- "If you want to grow your organization, you need to develop yourself to become a good leader."

"Having a good feeling" helps us to grow well. It helps keep things moving with more energy. A manager desperately needs such feelings. Having a good feeling enlivens a manager. Dr. Wayne Dyer stated in *The Power of Will*:

- *". . . change your mindset and have a mind that is ready to accept everything. Because this ability is granted only to you humans."*

Always be thankful to God Almighty.

Be grateful to be gifted with the opportunity to grow and excel. This gratitude is the source of good feelings that are strongly helpful. In the business world, it has been proven that successful people are both grateful and have high confidence and self-esteem. One of the best types of self-care is to first imagine yourself in the position you want. Then target it and commit yourself to attain it.

The partial good emotions (such as partial pieces of the puzzle of success) act as a driving force. This driving force is powerful. It is your Launchpad to the world of success.

One important thing to keep in mind is that we should not attribute our bad lives to God. Many people around the world make this mistake. This mistake will be the main cause of their destruction. Thank God that you have a healthy body and a reasoning mind.

John C. Maxwell says:

- "When it comes to personal growth, "action," says the last word."

Dr. Wayne Dyer also said:

- "The only thing I can be responsible for is my own personality."

Now, let's take a look at some of the backgrounds of good feelings (in the management world).

The best good feeling appears when we accept that we have a very important role to change our life for the better.

The best good feeling appears when we do not throw our tasks to other people's fields. The best good feeling appears when we plan for every day and know why we get out of the house today and what important things we need to do in the field of management. The best good feeling appears when we are sympathetic to the goals we have set. At this time, we will continue to grow with all of our hearts and souls. The good feeling is essential for a manager who has a plan. Managers who have good feelings also have an acceptable personality in the community. They have a lot of clients and there are many who are willing to fight for his cause.

Good feelings beget great personalities.

Napoleon Hill says:

- "There are many people with a variety of vague goals. But they do not get anywhere because they do not have the confidence to devise specific plans to achieve those goals."

We conclude this discussion with a nice statement by Jim Ran:

- *"It's a pity if your income has grown, but not yourself."*

GOOD LIFE

All of us humans have been born to live well. That is a principle. If we do not exercise this right, we have been unfaithful not only ourselves but also our future generations. We will be lasting for generations to come, if our existence benefits others too. The benefit that others can gain from us is very important. It will be a good life as long as our lives are toward growth and excellence and affect the excellence of others. The structure of a good life is to have good quality, if that is not the case then what do we live for? The main type of good life is growing life.

Life with purpose is also a good life. The same is true for a life with learning.

In the field of learning, we should mention the Spanish philosopher Baltasar Gracián y Morales:

- *"Find friends who teach you and mix the enjoyment of socializing with the benefits of learning."*

For a successful manager, it is a norm that he will have a good impact on the lives of others and have a good life of his own. To become immortal, think about expanding the good life.

Great people think of immortality.

An undeniable principle is that humans are created for one another and must help each other out.

All of us need to direct our lives toward the best examples. As well as having a positive impact on the lives of those around us.

The tree continues to grow as long as it lives. Put down these words somewhere. Tree, Growth, Life.

A good life is not just about having more wealth. A good undertaking and a good deed also contribute to creating a good life. A good life has deep truths that require careful consideration. From the perspective of every person, the facts are defined in a special way.

God says:

- *"It is only the wise who understand the truth."*

One of the sayings of the great Prophet of Islam (PBUH) is:

- *"The supremacy of the wise over the worshipper is like the superiority of the full moon over the other stars."*

Plato has an interesting statement:

- *"The teacher arrives when the student is ready."*

There are many people who complain about life! However, this is the life that should be complaining against them.

Do you know why? Because it is up to the individual to decide for his own life and the way to go. How does one expect life to care for him when he does not care for his own life? It is a pipe dream.

The care must be reciprocal. If we care for life, life will care for us too.

A quote from Jean Valjean in Victor Hugo's book, Les Misérables :

- *"Death is no big deal. Not to ever live is painful."*

Let us not forget that people who have somehow served the community have always been referred to as benevolent. They will last a long time of hundreds of years. Look at history to see the truth.

A good life is to recruit others to achieve our goals.

In this subject, managers have a wider scope of action than ordinary people in society.

Always keep in mind that usefulness, having high quality and learning spirit, purposefulness, ongoing growth, the satisfaction of the community, to serve, to help, and many other elements help us live a good life.

Focus on the learning spirit much more than other items. Because the more you know, the more you strive to make your life better.

Knowledge gives us power.

Admittedly, much of what we know has been learned from others. In fact, everyone's knowledge capacity is the sum of other people's knowledge capacity.

On helping others, it is noteworthy that it is also one of the imperative elements in building a good life that needs to be taken seriously. All of these elements are in different ways depending on our inner settings and personality structure. That is, what kind of spirit and moods do we have in building a good life? Work hard on this.

At the end of the discussion about one's inner virtues, we mention a good statement from Ramsay Thomson's book, Consciousness, and Creativity:

Management Clinic

– "The quality of your life depends largely on the quality of your inner emotions and mental life."

SPECIAL PEOPLE

It is not an exaggeration that ten percent of the world's population decides for ninety percent of the world's population. These ten percent are special people. Dealing with things that everyone is in control of is not a great feat. The genius is to swim against the direction of the flow. Special people have unique actions and reactions. Their life experiences are much different than those of ordinary people. The route they have chosen is a path less traveled by. Few people want to follow the eerie and risky path of special people.

Out of every hundred people, about ten to twelve think of valuable things such as purpose, commitment, practice, ideas, change, risk, perseverance, and action. The rest of those with a higher percentage are reluctant to accept such forbidding matters. Since these elements are essential to success, and success is not easy, thus they prefer a simple, down-to-earth life rather than a glorious and excellent one.

Just to decide to be a unique and one of a kind person is a great task in itself.

Special people are not afraid of failure. They convert all obstacles into opportunities to reap good and useful results. Clearly, fear of failure has captured the mind and soul of a large percentage of the world's population. If not for fear of failure, what magnificent accomplishments would people have?

A good statement from John Maxwell:

- *"If you do not turn your back to the difficult conditions that you are facing, you can find out its positive aspects."*

In fact, by a true understanding of being special, one can gain a huge reward. One cannot expect success from those who see failure as the end of life and who refuse to change their minds. They are always waiting for decisions that special people will make for them.

Special people, without fear of failure, are better off each day than yesterday. This is a characteristic of successful people.

How special are you in your life and managing your business?

To be special is to deal with things that no one else thinks about them. Things that not everyone can master. Sheldon Cup says:

- *"All important battles take place within a human being."*

Why are Charlie Chaplin, Picasso, Gandhi, Edison, Mandela and other influential people in the community considered special individuals? Because they were pioneers in their field of expertise. They did things that no one else was willing to do. The Prophet Jesus (PBUH) said:

- *"These are the unknown paths whose travelers are few."*

Special people are dependent on themselves more than their dependence on others. Dependence on others and governments is a characteristic of ever unhappy and forsaken people. Successful executives and individuals, who seek excellence, strongly avoid such affiliations and disturbing thoughts.

But let's see what factors are involved in being a special person? The first step to being special is to distance yourself from retarded people. The second step to be special is to think of ideas that no one else thinks about.

For special people, today is not the same as yesterday.

Stuart B. Johnson says:

- "Our purpose in life is not to overtake others, but to break our own records so that our today is not equivalent to our yesterday."

FUTURE GENERATIONS

I once asked a wealthy man the reason for his business success and excellence. He said:

- "…poverty was inherited from my great grandfather to my grandfather! It was inherited from my grandfather to my father and from my father to me! This generation-by-generation poverty had overshadowed our family and no one did anything to eradicate it. But due to disasters we suffered from poverty, I decided to halt its progress and do not allow it to take its toll from future generations. It is not fair that I also have a legacy of such a fateful inheritance."

Let us not forget that we leave many things behind and the future generations will benefit from them.

Basically, the one who is thinking about the future will also be thinking about the future generations, unlike the one who does not think about tomorrow and does not imagine a bright future for himself, and therefore, the life of the future generations will not matter to him either.

Remember, there are three types of responsibilities in our life cycle:

- Responsibility for ourselves
- Responsibility for the family
- Responsibility for future generations

We may have laughed at the quality of life of people who lived in the past (at their attitudes, clothing, dialogues) and the road traffic situation of a hundred years ago when funny cars roamed the streets, but can we laugh at the lives of people like Amir Kabir, Shah Abbas, Nader Shah, Karim Khan and the like?

The quality of life of great people in history is far more instructive and amazing than to be a laughingstock.

Even today's life seems rational in its own respect, but rest assured, there are some interesting things in this era that will be a laughingstock in the future. If future generations laugh at our lives, do you think it is right they laugh at me and you too?

The great and influential historical figures will never be ridiculed by future generations.

Any life we live today; we will see its impact in the future. Put aside the grievances and complaints and take action now. Let's make every moment full of joy and fundamental impact on our future generations.

I was sitting next to a successful person, owner of a restaurant chain in five locations. We talked about life and its quality and its impact on future generations. All of a sudden, I said to the restaurant owner:

- "I am pissed off with my father who did nothing for me."

By hearing that, the restaurant owner laughed and said:

- "It is true that your father did nothing for you, but you are not dead yet! *You* do something for your kids!"

If we are to accept that we are the founders of the lives that our children will accomplish, then we must consider that they need our today's purpose, creativity, planning, and effort, rather than our bank account deposit.

Let's not forget a simple tutorial book will be eventually forgotten, but a reference book will be passed down from generation to generation. So let's live our lives as a reference book for our children, not a simple educational booklet.

I remember a friend asked me:

- "Hey ... do you know your fourth, fifth, sixth and seventh great grandfathers?"

This question first got me confused. But after a short pause, I said:

- "Not really! I do not know who they were and what they did!"

My friend laughed and said:

- "So, clearly they were not important people! Otherwise, you would not forget their names! Influential people will never be forgotten from memories. Influential and important people will last for hundreds of years."

Let's have goals and plans that benefit us first and then our future generations.

Imam Ali (AS) said:

"If you are looking for salvation, be diligent and hard-working."

THANKFULNESS

Now, we want to talk about God, an infinitely transcendent being. The God whose holy being prevails over the universe and owns the heavens and the earth. Thank God for providing us with many opportunities to live and relate our lives to good things.

The lives of all of us humans are full of opportunities.

The lives of all of us humans are full of the possibilities that the Almighty God has provided for our success. He grants success as one of our rights and if there is an obstacle, He will remove it for us. God is rich and he wants us to be rich. God acknowledges that we deserve success. God believes in us and there is no basis for our success except this divine belief.

Let us not forget that there is no more valuable bond than our bond with our God. God loves us so much that He is even closer to us than the jugular vein. Such love is commendable. God, Himself said:

- "My servant, if you know how much I love you, you will pass away under this overwhelming cognition."

God has given common sense to me and to you to live well.

Somewhere I read:
- "Nothing is better than being thankful for what you have."
Thanksgiving opens the door to pure ideas.

Take a day to visit the disabled care center and even the mentally disabled center to realize the true nature of health and its value.

When I was a child, at a visit to such a center set up by the school, the instructor of the disabled hall said to us:
- "I want to transfer the garden I inherited from my father to one of your students!"

We were all surprised to hear this. One of my classmates said:
- "to who?"

The coach raised his right arm. Then he waved his index finger with a particular smile and said:
- "To a student who is willing to lose a finger!"

The coach's words had confused us all. At first, we did not understand what it meant, but after thinking for a while, we understood what the coach meant. No student was thrilled to hear the coach's condition. The coach broke the silence and said:
- "So neither of you are willing to make a fortune in exchange for losing a finger. It is true?"

We all said unanimously:
- "Yes..."

One of the kids said:
- "If you give me ten orchards, I am not willing to have a finger cut."

The coach lowered his arm and said:

- "Appreciate your health. People who are not physically healthy are kept in this center. Some actually are not mentally healthy. This has kept them away from many of the blessings. Health is so valuable that you do not even want to get rich in exchange for losing a finger."

There is no price for your life because the gift of God cannot be priced and more valuable than the gift of God, is the effort you make to direct it toward success. Every single day of the Lord's days is an opportunity. Every day is an opportunity for growth and excellence. These opportunities can be joyful. These are all blessings.

Opportunities can be a bridge between humans and the world of joy and excellence.

Imam Ali (as) says:

- "A time of joy and happiness is a good opportunity to refresh the soul."

Dr. Wayne Dyer says:

- "When you say 'thank you God for everything'; you show your respect for the creator of being."

The life of all of us humans is not a small part of the vast universe, but a large part of the universe. Let's not doubt this fact because God is flowing into our lives.

That amount of believability is enough to have a good life and for purpose and perseverance.

Catherine Pander has written:

- "Always remember that God is the source of all blessings. Then make spiritual contact with Him and His rich essence and rich aspirations that await your follow up."

Ask God whatever you want. To express this want, you need to rise. So, let's get up. The day we rise is a great day. The day

Management Clinic

that all successful people started from there.

POWER OF BELIEF

No one gives a damn for an ordinary manager. Everyone is eager to meet the top executive and listen to him. Never underestimate yourself, and use each of your potential talents in line with the goals of your organization. Your abilities are very high. Interestingly, the ability level with the believability level can both be strengthened and weakened. So, you have to work hard on your beliefs.

The principle of self-esteem is one of the most fundamental principles of success.

Lack of self-esteem has many ailments, including dependence on the trap of decisions of others, overwhelming fear of failure, to tolerate bad conditions and the loss of confidence.

What do you think is the difference between a simple headache and fatal cancer? Cancer is clearly much more destructive than a simple headache. Because it disrupts and kills a large part of the body limbs.

One who does not believe in himself (from a vulnerability perspective) is no different than a cancer patient.

This person has completely eliminated "confidence",

"mobility", "purposefulness", "motivation" and "willpower" (all of which are important elements in success). Naturally, when such valuable assets are wasted, there is nothing left of a man except a few pieces of flesh, skin, and bones! On the other hand, one who believes in himself has all his potentials boiling hot which lifts him up.

Self-esteem is, in essence, a source that can flow through all parts of our lives and usher in liveliness. This spring can create a sea of empowerment and success in our lives. We must not let this spring dry out.

A person who underestimates himself and tramples on his self-esteem is never qualified to sit on the management seat.

By believing in oneself and changing some of the components, success will be achieved. In the field of management, a manager is at the forefront of everything. In order for the organization to survive, he has to first start from himself. He has to believe in himself. This self-esteem must be institutionalized so much that he would survive the challenges of the business market.

Challenges such as supply and demand market fluctuations, political changes of governments and economic and financial crises.

The worst factor for a manager's bankruptcy in work is to be mired in a world of doubts.

Doubts about whether he would be believed or not?! With such doubts that are extremely destructive, the matters will either hardly progress or not at all. Doubts and suspicions must be removed from the miracle of self-esteem. We need to make changes in our components that will enhance our self-esteem, not to strike our own roots.

Changing some components is not about physical and bodily changes, but about fundamental changes in our thinking, as well as discarding destructive attitudes that (by destroying self-esteem) destroy our business.

Keep in mind that the way you can believe in yourself and by using the miracle of belief makes useful changes to your life and your future generations, others will not believe you as such. When a manager has self-esteem, that self-esteem (like the blood that runs through the veins) will be injected into the smallest parts of his organization and encompasses all the capacities of his organization.

John C. Maxwell has written somewhere:

- "If you want your organization to grow, you need to nourish yourself to become a good manager."

COMPETENCIES

The fact is that all people in society (depending on their abilities) have their own merits. Not everyone is deaf, blind, handicapped, or defective. Even the most disadvantaged people in society (even though they do not see themselves powerful) demand respect. The person who is incapacitated is not supposed to be offended, isolated and insulted. Whether some people are incapable of expressing their abilities or competencies depends on themselves, otherwise, all humans have an inner potential that can change the world. If such power lies in the heart of men, then one should never underestimate other people.

Basically, a person's competence (in a series of specific tasks) is revealed when the person portrays his abilities. In order to penetrate and gain a foothold in society, you must know that the majority of human beings deserve respect.

When we respect people who are welcomed and credited in the community, it means we have an understanding of competencies. Let us not forget that humans are the most capable creatures of the omniscient creator.

Catherine Pander argues:

- "All human beings can create what they imagine in their imagination."

If a person has the right to succeed, then others have the right to do so because all people are attached to the locus of divine power. Start the competencies from yourself. You, who have dignity and respect. Dr. Wayne Dyer has an thought-provoking statement:

- *"Disrespect for yourself is not only disrespect for one of the creatures, but disrespect for the creator."*

If one believes in one's own merits, one also believes in other people's competencies. Be sure some of the merits of others will help you a lot. One should not simply bypass merits.

The people who take their talents seriously are the victorious people of society.

Every person we have in our organization has many pros and cons. What is needed for our organizational growth and excellence are the positive aspects that others have?

Dr. Wayne Dyer has mentioned elsewhere:

- *"When you disregard others and look down on them, why should they help you?"*

In the past, the competencies and talents tool (due to an antiquated mentality) may have been troublesome, and the creative person was considered "incompatible" but today's society no longer thinks so and everyone is trying to show his merits. However, think about the competencies and make the most of the individual and collective merits.

Your organization is full of merit.

Your organization is full of people who are competent and capable in ways that may not come to your mind.

A successful organization is a meritocratic organization. An organization where each individual (from management to the lowest administrative level) is positioned based on competencies. The downturn and stagnation of an organization occur when the "principle of competence" is swept under the rug.

A competent manager also has competent thoughts.

Competent thoughts beget competent insights and attitudes. The competent organization will have countless customers and clients. Competencies and consideration of meritocracy will lead you to build a brand and become pricier. Do not miss this.

INDIVIDUAL POWER, COLLECTIVE POWER

It is not farfetched if we say that no one can do everything on his own (even though he is very capable). No matter how powerful an individual is, it does not match the power and extent of collective power. However, the same individual power is a valuable privilege in its own right which must be taken into account.

Consider a supermarket. A well-equipped supermarket, no matter how much potential it has and good services it provides still lacks the revenue-generating power of a chain store with many branches. These separate branches are the collective power of the supermarket owner that makes him wealthy. There is a well-known saying in the market as follows:

- "More branches beget more opportunities."

More branches mean a lucrative collective power that will guarantee a high income. A manager is not supposed to use all of his power to advance things on his own. If that was true, so what is the use of human and personnel resources?

It has always been a character of the staff that they want to be seen and do something to promote their organizations and establishment. They like to be involved in the collective power of the organization. If you do not have such a belief as a manager, you will not go anywhere.

An example, a concept:

The manager number is "one" and the following sequence is "zero"... for example, you as a manager will be powerful with ten people: 10,000,000,000. That is the secret to the power of a manager. Converting individual power into collective power.

Or a simpler example with a question:

Are the numbers $1 + 1 + 1 + 1 + 1 + 1$ stronger or number 6?

(Think a moment before answering this question.)

The answer is simple. It is natural that the number 6 is much stronger than the six separate ones. In this example, we are dealing with a topic called "organizational synergy". Your organization needs to reach a single number in planning and policymaking rather than trying to do tasks separately and individually. This is the true meaning of collective power.

There is no reason for a manager to be self-centered and a lone wolf. An organization could be run by several people or by a powerful manager, but the organization will not always remain so small. Your organization grows, and consequently, it needs to expand its mental and collective power.

John Edder says:

- *"The more you allow others to contribute to matters; it will be more likely that the matters will get better."*

The more you believe in and exploit the power of your staff and those around you; you will be a better winner. To increase workloads, effort, and profitability, believe that others can do many things for you.

There are many people who love you and many people believe your attitudes. Many of these people like your character and many like your plans. Such people can help strengthen your work team and increase your collective strength.

Ignoring collective power makes the path to success and wealth very difficult.

If someday, your staff arrives at the workplace with the hope of a salary and pension and your organization's goals are worthless to them, your organization will be a disgusting, fragile and unstable establishment. Certainly, such a sick organization will only get worse every day. The personnel must work with love and interest in work, to advance the organization with the hope that they are respected and valued. The collective power needs these things. If the human resources of an organization think about the organization's goals and move in the right direction, the success of that organization is guaranteed.

Remember, dissatisfied personnel is most eager to destroy the company and organization, and this is the biggest plague in the business world. John Edder states in his book *Creative Thinking*:

- *"Everyone who works for you has ten thousand million brain cells. If you have the time, it is good to listen to what others say. Then you will be amazed at the high quality of the ideas and thoughts available to you."*

Steve Jobs had said somewhere:

- *"All Apple company employees think about one goal."*

A strong manager is not a manager who uses 100 percent of his power, but a manager who uses one percent power of one hundred people. You will succeed when you attract and develop powerful people in your company and organization and direct them toward a specific goal. One day at a success seminar, a successful entrepreneur told me:

- *"I am not worried about leaving my company for a year. Because some of my staff are better than me. I am certain that all the agents are one and the same and think about one goal. I attribute my success to this kind of empathy and teamwork."*

Dear Manager!

A secret to win in the business world is to have far more powerful people than yourself around you, and the second is to make good use of those powerful people.

RELIANCE

Let us first mention a nice statement by Catherine Pander that says:

- *"Free your mindset from shortcomings and scarcity and believe that this world is rich and full of blessings. Just for you and me. Why not rely on the God who created such a world?"*

Reliance on God strengthens the heart. But reliance on a God's servant is not that strong.

A seven or eight-month-old infant can get up by leaning on the wall. Having suitable support allows the baby to increase its stamina. "Deciding to do something" is the first step and "moving" is the second step. So where reliance comes into the equation?

One of the spiritual leaders has an interesting statement:

- *"Every human movement will be continued if it is attached to the divine center."*

Without reliance on God, there is a defect in the work.

Without reliance on the holy divine being, the sense of emptiness will be felt in the work process, and without reliance, man will not have powerful support for his work.

Without reliance on God, every effort in life pales out and loses it robustness.

Relying on the holy divine being boosted the light of hope.

Reasoning and aware mind know that God is the main source of power and ability, and we must ask help only from Him. Therefore, all his activities are hopefully tied to Him. If it is God's will to give you a share of this world, then He will not leave you alone.

Dear Manager!...

Rely on God, not to the amount of effort, desires you have, but more than the effort, and desires you have. The climber who is tied to a strong nail climbs up with ease. We all know that without the proper equipment we cannot reach the summit.

The best equipment to climb in life is to rely on God!

Do not forget to rely on God since you will have to endure bad conditions. Management and management methods, when they are tied to the principle of the existence of God and reliance on Him, become the most robust type of management. So, we conclude that for excellence and success we must provide the undeniable capacity of "reliance on the holy divine being" in our lives and businesses.

WILLPOWER

"Will" means a strong intention to go along with a decision to achieve a certain outcome. All humans have the potential for both "free will" and "willpower", but the level of believability of these two tools is not the same in everyone.

When we trust in the will power, we must also be ready to accept God's help.

The willpower does let your inner forces stand still and keeps them in perpetual motion. In an apple blossom, there is no apple, but the same apple blossom becomes an apple by connecting to the willpower. The will power converts a drop into a fetus and directs the fetus on the path of growth. The willpower exists around us and in all parts of the being. Therefore, certainly, it is inside you too (the reader of this book).

A Chinese short story . . .

One day a dragon asked a centipede:

- "How do you put together so many legs? I hardly sort out my legs!"

The centipede replied:

- "Honestly, it's not me that is keeping together my legs!"

The willpower is linked to the absolute power of God.

By appealing to the willpower, you will have a far greater force than an atomic bomb that can transform the world. The will power can create a strong attraction.

For example, if you have wishes like an ordinary person throughout the normal life of, adapt to the environment, and spend the day, you will attract the mundane phenomena of life. It is clear that you can get whatever you want. Undoubtedly, you have been instrumental in shaping what you are now. That is why they say:

- "People's personality is the result of their thinking."

Leo Tolstoy writes about his fictional hero, Ivan Ilyich:

- "... Ilyich's life story is very trivial and ordinary. So it is very hard and terrible..."

It really is. A trivial, dull, ordinary and boring life must be a very difficult and terrible life. If God's omnipotence is not ordinary and mundane and it is constantly growing and producing new phenomena and giving infinite blessings, why should the will power look for pipe dreams and dull ordinary life? Is not this kind of attitude unfaithfulness to our future generations? Guy Finley wrote in the book Determine Your Fate Yourself:

- "... All that exists on Earth indicates enormous energy. Whether stone or soil and mud, I or you..."

Willpower can deliver us from an imposed life and achieve the conditions we desire. Willpower must be taken seriously. Jim Ran says:

- *"The language of the will is I will."*

A determined person says:

- *"I will climb this mountain!"*

Others talk about the difficulties of the route and the steep valleys and downhills, but he replies:

- "It is my job. You will either see me on the summit soon, or I will die under effort!"

When we have willpower, we can do a lot of things. Events happen around us that are beyond our control and willpower, but what about the reaction to them. Are we not in control of a part of what is happening around us? And the last word:

When the willpower can provide us with good things, then from today we should focus our thoughts on good things.

INNER FORCE

Humans can turn to an active volcano from a dormant volcano. A human is no different from a volcano. The volcano mountain has a restless and wild nature. Forces like thought, free will, willpower, decision, desire, and ability, each of which can, in turn, transform the world, shape the inner essence of man.

Remember, what adds to the glory of the volcano is sweltering. An unstable state of affairs rooted in a restless soul, otherwise, no one cares about dormant volcanoes that would be quickly forgotten.

Sometimes a person is great at thinking and making decisions but reluctant in action.

Sometimes a person has many desires but does not move in line with fulfilling his wishes or taking action for his desires. There are people who do crazy things if they want to, but in the course of their lives, their willpower diminishes! On the other hand, there are people who cap their willpower or sell it to others free! That is, they have no free will and others are the main decision-makers in their lives!

None of the above qualities is of any use and successful people have no such characteristics. The "inner forces" are very valuable and are not sold at any store.

If you tell an ordinary person in a society that, he does not have the right to think and make decisions, or even the right to choose, the world will turn dark for him and imagines himself in a prison! He knows very well that thinking, free will, choice, decision, willpower, and desire are his most valuable assets.

Every person has the talent to make great changes in the world, provided he says *yes* to his inner forces. Consider also that achieving the wishes is subject to payment of compensation.

In principle, the personnel will not listen to a manager who has neither willpower nor the authority by himself and does not think reasonably, nor are his decisions rational.

All the efficiency of an organization depends on the power of the manager of the complex, and the power of a manager depends on a good understanding of his inner forces. Write these six options: *Thinking, Willpower, and Free Will, Decision, to Want* and *To Be Able* somewhere and assess for yourself in which one of them you excel?

SERIOUS DETERMINATION

Basically, the person who is serious in doing something has probably considered the aspects of the job, or else he will not take a firm step forward. Powerful people in society have relied on the powerful force of willpower and take their steps. This kind of step taking requires serious determination.

Doing simple things is not a serious determination. A serious determination needs serious people.

Serious determination has many challenges and ups and downs that can lead to failure at times, but its output is not bad. A rewarding experience cannot be traded with any wealth. All the serious and society-building developments of humanity have resulted from a serious determination.

A foot leaves no footprint of itself unless the foot takes firm steps.

Any effective and strong moves you make will have good outcomes. You dear Manager put a serious determination behind your decisions. You will never be useful and effective if anyone who arrives influences your decisions and overshadows your determination.

An effective and determined manager will have a lot of followers.

It is interesting to know that one of the interesting characteristics of the staff is that they (unlike common belief) prefer a serious and determined manager to a sluggish and lazy manager who is not determined.

If your organization breaks into several pieces of managerial action, it cannot identify right from wrong. In an economic crisis (which is always possible), the manager's determination is diluted with chaotic and diverse ideas, and he is forced to give up the control of the situation and eventually a profiteering power takes over.

The secret to the company or organization's survival lies in its practical cohesion and serious determination.

You must work seriously to correctly get through the challenges. Think about it from now on. Is it possible that a child does not get sick? Your organization is your baby. Just as a father goes to great lengths as soon as he finds out his baby is sick and takes it to the nearest clinic without pause and delay, you must show such a determination as well.

Do not sit idle in the face of social issues and complexities and be serious about them. Some prudent managers (using a consulting room) work based on the collective and rational determination. Should not a good manager keep a number of wise and thoughtful advisors around him, rather than hearsay and listening to biased opinions of any freak, and take serious action with the review of the subject matter?

Unfortunately, (due to long tenor) sometimes a manager is not committed to the collective determination. This by itself be the grounds for failure. Remember, most of the time consultants are ahead of managers. Not practically, but scientifically. A manager is responsible for the job, and a consultant is responsible for the expertise of the job.

Basically, a counselor is needed to reduce anxiety and avoid doubt. If a manager succumbs to lingering doubts, his decision will not be firm enough. When you are determined to do the right thing, move quickly without looking back.

No runner looks back because it is possible that the other runners overtake. The runner speeds up as he looks forward. In the world of competition and business, the organization under your command is also a runner. It must move forward and look forward to your serious determination and does not stop for a moment.

You have increased your credibility if your work as a knowledgeable manager is based on the serious determination. You look like a concrete wall that one can safely rely on. When the staff is leaning against a concrete wall, no hurricane can break them apart. It is the clay and straw plastered walls that collapse or slip down with any drizzle or mild wind.

A consistent and determined manager is a manager with a strong determination to do the job. The serious manager keeps the organization under his control inside his concrete fence.

SELF-ESTEEM

You have to nurture yourself to become a good manager. If you want a better child, you have to be a better person. Most of your people and those around you do not realize that you are a capable and talented person, and they do not care what the level of your growth and success is.

Samuel Silver says:

- "The biggest miracle is that tomorrow; we do not have to be the person who we are today."

If we believe in ourselves, and use all talents that God has put in us, we can improve. You have to believe in yourself and identify your abilities. Around you, people's advice is more deterrent than progressive. The public speaks of failures, shortcomings, misfortunes, problems, and pains, rather than victories and successes! So, sometimes it is necessary to be deaf to the destructive advice of others! Of course, not at all times.

Edison's hearing loss became an effective factor in minimizing the negative impacts and destructive advice of those around him and he continued to practice and work by believing in his own capabilities.

Edison was well aware that his beliefs were of no value to others! But did he have such a perception of himself? Ultimately, these powerful beliefs made him one of the few influential people in the world. This miracle of belief and power exists in "self-esteem".

Dr. Spencer Johnson says:

- *"You can control your personal peaks and valleys through your beliefs and actions."*

A story...

Once upon a time, two frogs with short and long jumps were moving through an area. Suddenly both fell into a deep hole! The only way to save themselves was the long jumps they could make. But no matter how they tried, they could not get out of the pit. At this moment, a number of frogs came to the edge of the hole, watching the endless efforts of those two frogs from above. When the frogs at the edge of the hole saw their dire circumstances, they shouted and yelled to make the two frogs realize that it was impossible to get out and save their asses! Do not try in vain! The best way is to surrender to death!

The first frog was convinced by the advice of frogs and crawled into a corner until his death arrives! But the second frog kept on trying and finally, got out of the pit with a long jump! All the frogs encircled it by seeing the boldness and diligence of the second frog. At this moment, the frogs realized that the rescued frog is deaf! In fact, the rescued frog thought the frogs at the edge of the pit were cheering it on (contrary to the reality) by shouting and yelling! While it was not so!

So, as mentioned before, it is sometimes necessary to be deaf to the destructive suggestions of others. Finally, let's have a look at the "miracle of belief"…

When we say "miracle", it means something that many people fail to produce. When we say "miracle of belief", we mean to reach the highest level of faith and belief. Few people achieve the highest level of belief and faith, and fewer reach the stage to believe in themselves as a wonderful being.

That is why we need to use the word "miracle" to understand the importance of faith and belief in talents and abilities, and to say that someone who has such strong faith is a true miracle worker.

Human beings have been the main cause of many changes and progress, but not all human beings, only those who believed in themselves as an amazing earthling. They have discovered their capabilities and potentials, and have come up with inventions, discoveries and innovations (to change existing conditions).

You also have to believe in yourself to change conditions and grow. Believe in all your limbs and bones. Believe in all your moods and attitudes.

If you have a disability, believe in other fully working limbs of your body. By believing all these components, you will also believe in the universe and eternal power. When all of these components come together, a powerful being like a human being is created and then the miracle is possible.

Success comes with believing in oneself and changing some of the components.

THE RULER – THE RULED

In the business world, we are confronted with two issues: one is "ruling" and the other "obedience". A successful ruler is a ruler who expands his business geography.

The rulers think of growth.

The rulers do not like to stop.

The rulers demand escalation.

The rulers are never afraid.

The rulers see themselves on the frontline.

The rulers always create unity.

It is a long way from ruling to the being ruled. Each has its own characteristics and scope.

A ruling is a transcendent and farsighted quality that not everyone can attain. Ruling in business requires skill, courage, risk-taking power and many other attributes that are beyond other people's reach.

The rulers think far ahead and have long-term plans for themselves. They have not come to go back soon. They have come to stay long and affect the lives of others. Most great entrepreneurs are such people. Most of the great and successful executives who have established a cohesive and growing organization with their knowledge and expertise are such people. Get ready to rule.

Capture the business market so you are not caught up in the business.

You cannot call yourself a ruler unless you have a certain percentage of impact on the market and business circulation. Rulers are influential in the business market and in the process of business and management, and their decisions are very effective.

If you take a look at the lives of successful people in the community and ambitious executives who have influenced the business world, you will find that those people had big plans and goals. Having a big plan is not everyone's piece of cake. Many go astray in achieving their goals, but not the rulers.

Now let's talk about the ruled. An "obedient" person has no sense of independence. He is somehow a tool for the ruler to achieve his goals. We see many examples of this in the business world. Decide today to be the leader of your business and expand your business geography. Because in the world of obedience you will be the first victim of history.

The real victim is someone who is quickly forgotten at the speed of light in every page of history. Because he does not accomplish anything. The ruled are of this category but not the rulers. Think about it well and set your boundaries.

- "There is a difference between a soldier and a commander."

The major difference between a commander and a soldier is in the scope of authority.

There are many differences between the one giving the order and the one taking the order. Work well on understanding these differences to gain a broader knowledge about ruling the people.

Growth and excellence

There is a fact in the business: "Work minus growth is a rat race."

Your success comes when you grow every day.

Your mind's stagnation will render your organization immobile. The power of work is in growth and excellence. Do not let your mind sink into a standstill since you will be afflicted with occupational immobility. As your mind shuts down, your business shutters will also be pulled down. The mind's stagnation is means giving the opportunity to competitors to grow and surpass you. This overtaking will destroy you.

If the mind and the work's stagnation is far from growth and excellence, the customer will be tired of you. Customer fatigue is equal to your bankruptcy.

Do not stop. Stay current. Follow through. Rivers that are clear and flowing are always a delight to passersby.

When your plans are continuously being implemented, it means that your organization is lively and growing. Do not put a barbed wire fence around the growth and excellence of your business. Work and growth are possible everywhere. Because the human mind has no specific framework and can crystallize beyond what is conjectured. If you define a limit for your growth and excellence, you have reduced your development and progress.

Development and progress know no limits. If you are constantly chewing the same old gum, you are doomed to retreat. There is no benefit, wealth, and excellence in going backward and retardation. I heard this from a successful executive:

- "Unless the change is mingled with growth and excellence, customers will no longer come to you. Customers, although they do not accept change on steroids, like gradual change. Growth is always related to change."

"Movement and change" are complementary. The right balance must be struck between them. Share your growth method with your organization. There are many people who suggest you interesting ideas. Do not enclose yourself in the shell of your capacity. Use others too. Others can be a useful element in your growth and excellence. Do not underestimate them.

Occasionally, other people's plans open our eyes wider on the path of growth and excellence. Our key point is to identify the individuals, groups, and organizations that will help you achieve better growth . . .

- People related to business
- Family members
- People unrelated to business

Write down this famous statement somewhere:

- The market gives the best rewards to the best growth."

The personality of a manager

It is a fact . . . the only thing I can be responsible for is my own personality. Our own personality must have substance and be taken care of.

Managers take care of their personalities.

People who play with their personality will certainly not appreciate the personality of others. However, what do you think is the best type of consolidating a personality?

One of the factors that consolidate and strengthens the personality is that we do not seek a culprit for failures and retardation.

Do not blame others for our downfall. Instead of expecting from others, we must expect from ourselves. The manager's personality must be dignified and respectful. In a manager, nothing is as interesting to the public as his personality.

Successful business executives always strive to enhance their personality. The manager's personality must be managerial. That is, his behavior, speech, and deeds must have a unique characteristic. The manager's personality can influence the structure of an organization and reveal the strengths and weaknesses of the establishment. Above all, we have to check what our managerial personality is. First from our own perspective and then from the perspective of others.

How much does this personality worth? Does it have any buyer at all? Is this personality progressive or deterrent? How much is it tied to the principle of honesty, the principle of sincerity, and the principle of ethics? How much is our personality worth? That value will be the value of our organization. In order to refine our personality, let's put ourselves in the spotlight of criticism.

Let's see what others think of us? Let them criticize us that some part of your behavior is defective. No problem. If we accept such criticisms and seek reform, our personality will be on the path to excellence. Whenever I met a successful person, I learned an interesting point from him (in terms of character recognition).

Successful people:

- Criticize themselves more than others.

(Are you open to criticism?)

- They are constantly engaged in new endeavors.

(How much are you involved in new efforts?)

They highly believe in themselves.

(Do you believe in yourself as much as it is necessary and appropriate?)

- They go to any lengths.

(How much do you try to get out of the maze of problems?)

- They liberate themselves from the umbrella of dependence.

(Have you thought about your intellectual and practical independence?)

- They bring up themselves purposefully.

(Do you have a vision for yourself?)

- They consider themselves incomplete.

(How long do you keep going?)

- They trust in themselves.

(How much is your self-confidence?)

The people who wait for others to do something for them are insignificant people who will never achieve the worthy desires and goals that they develop in their minds. Since the personality of a manager is very important, it is necessary to pay attention to the above.

MANAGER'S PRICE

Set a price for yourself. The manager's price sets the price of the organization. Why are many crisis-stricken companies willing to pay millions of dollars to hire self-made executives? Because the making of that executive leads to the revival of a company under crisis.

Dear Manager!

More important than determining the product price, company price and the price of human resources, is your own price.

Because the criterion for measuring an organization is the manager of that organization, when you are aware of your price, you will try to become even more expensive than your current price. A guerilla warfare general argues:

- "You should always be on the offensive. A trench should never be dug for defense."

Pricy managers are always on the offensive. Imagine yourself as an expensive person and try to make your assumption come true because you deserve the victory. If you believe in yourself otherwise, you will not get anywhere. You and your inner self have many potentials to bring you closer to your goals.

If you want your organization to grow, you need to grow first. Imam Ali (AS) says:

- "A person who is his own teacher and mentor deserves more respect than someone who is the teacher and mentor of others."

All of these words and statements by the great people deserve contemplation and must be applied. Increase your capacity to accept and receive business advice from great people to become more valuable. You need to know more and practice more.

FORCE OF THE UNIVERSE

There are forces around us that are counting seconds to fulfill our desires. Simply put, every person in his life has a magical and invisible Genie to achieve his goals. If we have little faith in this magical Genie, it would be less likely to help us.

The great force of the universe, in its true position, is like a magical Genie capable of fulfilling the wishes we have in our mind.

Any wish, if it is a real desire, will be converted to the ability of fulfillment. Wealth and prosperity is a fundamental right for all. Because the God of this world is rich and He wants each one of us to be rich and remain rich. Because God has created this rich world for our optimal use.

Remember that wealth, health and fortune are potentially within us. They just need to be converted to reality. The force of the universe must be used to actualize the inner forces and achieve the bliss.

If the sciences of physics, mathematics, music, and other sciences have specific laws, the force of the universe has its own rules too. If one can attract something to oneself by the mind, intellect, thought, mental imagery and the words (relating to that thing), so the force of the universe is a definite and real force and must be accepted as an undeniable principle and law.

There are many things in the imagination that allow you to attract the force of the universe.

"Imagination" brings the force of the universe to a boil.

One must exploit the power of imagination. In your imagination, which is the driving force behind the universe, imagine the things that you truly want, not the things you may be able to achieve. After a while, "imagination" takes over and employs the enormous force of the universe to achieve that desire.

The force of the universe is connected to the sacred treasure of God and will never leave you empty-handed.

Shakespeare has an interesting statement in this regard:

- "Human affairs are like tidal waves that drive them to fortune through the flood."

When you arrive at the workplace, begin to review your imagination and your sincerest wishes. If you are not supposed to be satisfied with the status quo to succeed, put growth on your agenda. Right now, imagine a great company and organization in your imagination and keep yourself entertained with it.

Imagination and mental imagery will use the force of the universe to make your plans come true, and all the elements and tools will be provided for you automatically. Basically, is it possible to get to a place you had never imagined before?

Suppose a student wants to become a teacher. Well, during

his student years, a teacher's job is the empty gap in his life and when he achieves his goal, the hole will be filled. We call this whole the "vacuum in life".

It is better not to forget that the vacuum in life is filled with the things that shape our desires. Since the force of the universe abhors a vacuum, so the vacuums of our lives will quickly be filled. For you, dear manager (in the business world), higher status, job excellence, greater wealth and economic growth and prosperity are considered a vacuum.

If you have such a gap and vacuum, be sure that it will be filled with connection to the force of the universe. I have met many low level and simple executives and I have finally discovered a secret. That is, the reason for the inferior managers' lack of growth was satisfaction with the existing conditions and the lack of a business vacuum. They thought everything was adequate and no longer dreamed of growth. Just like that.

Let's not forget that a manager who does not think about growth and excellence will not benefit himself or others.

The law of the universe is based on growth, movement, and excellence and it is ready to serve our progress. The important thing is to want and want and want. Management without mental development is incomplete management. It fails in every aspect. Management without mental growth is defective management. Management without a vision will be stagnant and commonplace management. Success and victory are achieved without excuses. A competent manager thinks of escalation. Only escalation.

Catherine Pander has written in the book *The Law of Wealth*:
- "When you see yourself as a successful and empowered person, you really help yourself to become that person."

Prosperity and wealth, growth, escalation and excellence . . . think about these things and keep engaging with them. God wants you to do the same and puts the force of the universe at your disposal to fulfill them. Just connect with God's rich blessings (this abundant ingredient and treasure chest).

THOUGHTFULNESS

Suppose someone with the name Ahmad walks with his head down. Walking like that makes it possible for Ahmad to hit many obstacles and objects. Or suppose Ahmed walks with his head raised up. This raised up posture also poses risks for Ahmad. He may not see the pit underfoot and fall into the hole. On the other hand, another person walks looking directly forward. Clearly, there is no possibility that this second person hits the obstacles, or (if he walks quickly) it will be less likely. In any case, he is walking the path correctly.

In the field of business, consider these three parables. The second person has forethought and prevents the incident before it happens, but Ahmad does not.

"Manager's thoughtfulness" means identifying the crisis before it occurs.

The situation is not always going to be the same. Never forget this. Believing that things will not always be the same is coming from your foresight, and you have reached the right level of thoughtfulness. You are actually ready to cross the barriers easily.

Thinking about the consequences is not the same for all managers. Some executives are heavily involved in bad and destructive thoughts in their minds (in terms of future events), which means the manager's pessimism and striking one's own roots! Such managers spread bad ideas (which will lead to bad waves) in the structure of the organization and cause their organization to collapse. This negativity and bad thoughts are not thoughtfulness; it is a deadly poison that is extremely damaging.

But elsewhere, there is a manager who develops good ideas in his mind and quickly finds solutions (before the crisis occurs) with making the right decisions. That means thoughtfulness.

One day I was the guest of a reputable newspaper's editor. During our talk, the newspaper circulation was mentioned. The editor, in reply to my question that why they do not increase the newspaper circulation, said:

- *"There is no need to increase. We will decrease over time! The number of people who browse the Internet and virtual networks is increasing daily and society is changing. In the not-too-distant future, the paper will be replaced by web pages. Why should we spend on increasing circulation? While newspaper sales are down due to Internet access. We have to foresee the future and be ready right now and make the right decision."*

The editor's answer was an example of true thoughtfulness and foresight. A manager needs to see himself in the future and make a decision right now. A strong manager should imagine his own situation, his organization's situation, services, products, and other organizational issues in the future.

A strong manager must always keep himself ready for escalation and change.

Think carefully before making any decision to keep your business going strong. Why do you think so many of the world's great industrial tycoons and companies were destroyed after a long time of leadership? Because they had no foresight. The failed and bankrupt managers of the past knew that the world was changing, but they refused to accept change and were not ready to face the crisis.

What do you think is the reason for building the attic on the upper floor of a building? Is it not for safety reasons against rain and snowfall? Thoughtfulness requires you to consider tomorrow and be fully aware of future conditions and possibilities. A capable manager thinks about tomorrow, sees himself in tomorrow, and plans for tomorrow. Thoughtfulness is a complementary and technical part of management.

A dumb manager is no different from a simple worker or a low-level employee.

Workers and employees in your organization are for running a daily business according to plan, but the manager has come to plan tomorrow's tasks besides the day-to-day tasks. This requires thoughtfulness. An employee has plans for today's organization and a manager for tomorrow's organization.

"Foresight" is a prerequisite for the success of a manager.

A manager must dig the matters. He must predict market volatility. He must be at least a few days ahead of time. "Thoughtfulness" makes the manager ready to face a vague tomorrow.

A thoughtful manager always assumes that he is flawed and delayed. This sense of backwardness will always keep him alert. If he thinks he has already been completed and the plans do not need to be upgraded, he will soon fail.

Never think you are perfect. You will never get anywhere with this idea.

DECISION-MAKING

One day, someone asked a wealthy man:
- "What was the secret to your success?"
The rich man replied:
- "Sound decisions."
He asked:
- "What was the cause of the sound decisions?"
The rich man replied:
- "Experience."
He asked:
- "What was the cause of gaining experience?"
The rich man replied:
- "Wrong decisions."

Decision-making defines your organization's life and death. Decision-making is very important in the process of business, but when it comes to action, it is different.

A decision is worthless unless it is implemented. Every human being makes dozens or hundreds of decisions during the month, but which one is really implemented?

It is a long way from words to action. Managers and business owners are overwhelmed with decision-making. Therefore, they must be extremely careful in making decisions.

Undoubtedly, the decisions of managers, in general, are based on growth and development because the secret to an organization's survival is change, growth, and development. Before making any decision, choose an idea that will trigger good feelings in you.

You have to keep good things in mind to get good results.

Good and sound decisions are the result of good and sound thoughts. Perhaps others and wise counselors will be able to assist you in conveying good ideas in various ways. That is fine, but as Jim Ran puts it:

- "Make your decisions based on your own conclusions."

It is up to you what you want to do. It is up to you to decide to be something or not to be. Just remember what you can do if you use your full potential.

The growth of an organization's manager depends heavily on the decisions you make.

A manager in the decision-making world is really going to wage war on himself. Based on the current economic conditions, the managers are continuously trapped in their vicious circle of 'What should I do? What should I do?' Therefore, they must be extremely careful in making decisions. Remember that managers are more likely to suffer from wrong decisions than the staff. Because they are the arrowhead and in the focus of the attention of others.

The rightness or wrongness of any decision overshadows your future career.

It is the quality of decision making that determines how

much you depend on others. Now we want to address the topic of "others". If it is supposed that the others make decisions for your organization, then what is your role as a manager?

Each manager is either under his own command or under the command of others. The main problem in decision-making will make a real sense at a time that you have no control over yourself and others have control over you. So, please do not imagine any bright prospects for yourself! Mastering the decisions by oneself can facilitate the principle of decision-making.

The manager in charge of the affairs, and especially of his own circumstances, make the decision easily. A dependent manager who has no authority by himself and others define his policy is actually a signature machine. Always frustrated and confused ...

The most obvious type of decision-making is about the type of organization you want to have. Successful people think well (before making any decision) and make the right decisions based on the facts surrounding them.

Mingle your decisions with two things:

- Innovation

- Follow up

A successful manager makes interesting, new and pristine decisions.

A successful manager will move decisions toward the achievement of the results. Dear Manager!... If you decide to have something that you have not yet, you should do something you have not done yet.

RECEIPT AND DELIVERY

If we take a closer look around, we will find that there is a wealth of experience, information, and knowledge around us.

(As a manager) how eager are you to get this knowledge and experience? We have said before that no one is completely perfect. A deficiency exists in all, and it is a deficiency that provides the motivation for learning.

You need to learn more to know more. Because knowledge helps, you make the right decisions. Anyone who knows more will grow more. Access the up-to-date information around you by any means and stay up to date. Keep on receiving knowledge and information.

Learn more about your work, your industry, and your products.

Do not deprive yourself of the source of knowledge and education. The more you know, the more successful you will be and the better decisions you will make. John C. Maxwell has written somewhere:

- "Life is harder for the people who have given up on growing, receiving and learning."

Remember, if we want to climb to the highest peak, we cannot expect to be successful overnight unless we have the necessary skills. In the business world, you will always face this question: 'What is the best solution?'

To learn more, you must have more than enough receiving power.

Develop yourself as an insatiable person to receive the volume of awareness. Most decisions based on inexperience and ignorance lead to failure. Although failure is not the end, it is better if you are more mature before the failure occurs.

The best strategy for making the right decision is to receive other people's experiences and talking with them. Someone who receives well will deliver well too.

The manager of a spaghetti company, using comments by a few planes Jane but innovate housewives, decided to create exquisite designs to change the popular shapes of spaghetti. This is called a good and clever reception. Although those housewives may not have been experts in the fields of economics, commerce, and market, they certainly had the necessary expertise in macaroni cooking and recognizing the tastes and wishes of the people.

Use all the empirical and practical elements around you to make the right decisions.

Every day a lot of frequencies are transmitted toward you. A clever and thoughtful manager attracts the frequencies that contain new and fresh ideas. Receive harsh criticism too. What is wrong with knowing about your problems and weaknesses?

Is it bad if someone tells you that your shirt collar is stuck under the coat collar? Powerful managers construct buildings with the bricks that are thrown at them.

Criticism, complaints, warnings, guidelines, suggestions, plans, good words, bad words and in summary, there are many things that flow toward you throughout another day. Receive all of them to make better decisions. Do not forget this sentence:

- "Gold seekers sometimes found gold in bowls full of mud and sludge of rivers and marshes."

Develop a decision in the bowl of receipts so that it is fully matured. The more capacity you have to receive, the clearer your mind engine and the wiser your decisions will be.

On the other hand, a manager is not supposed to include opinions of all other people in his decisions. In that case, he will get out of order and the situation is disrupted. What we mean by "receiving" is receiving knowledge and information around us (with great intelligence) and applying it in line with the decisions.

Story:

... One day a bankrupt and outcast manager was sitting on a bench in a park. At this moment, a boy with a plastic ball came up and sat down beside the manager. The boy realized the manager's anxiety and commented:

- "You look so sad!"

The manager initially ignored it, but the repetition of that question and the boy's persistence went so far that it forced the manager to start talking:

- "I have a match manufacturing plant. I went bankrupt. There is no hope left for me!"

The boy paused for a while and then came up with an

interesting reply:

- "You can make the matchbox so that the matching cover is printed on its back!"

The bankrupt manager asked:

- "What is the reason for this? So what?"

The boy said:

- "People are accustomed to using a matchbox with its cover upwards. When you print the cover upside down, all matchsticks will fall as soon as the matchbox is opened! Not everyone is patient enough to collect all the matchsticks. Then he will buy another matchbox! This is how the matches are going to sell!"

By hearing this tip, the bankrupt manager jumped up as if electrocuted and rushed toward his matchmaking factory!

PROCRASTINATION

Basically, one of the worst things that result in stagnation and standstill is "sitting idle". When a manager makes the right decision in his field of management, he must push that decision forward until the outcome is achieved.

Inaction, sitting idle and delay will slow you down.

We asked some executives why they were indecisive:

- "We are prudent!"

Although prudence is logical, prudence is a disadvantage when the decision is right. The right decision must be implemented immediately because it is right. Especially decisions that contain new ideas and plans. One day, leading hygiene industry executives wrote to me:

- "…during ten meetings with my expert advisors, we worked on an interesting idea about paper tissue production and concluded that in a certain week we must get the patent of our pristine idea and then implement it. Hoping that pristine idea will drive more sales and increase company revenue. But, due to too much clutter and excessive delay, a competitor company patented our idea in its own name and the idea simply got out of our reach. We were left with nothing but regret and stress. I wish our right decision would have not fallen victim to our procrastination . . ."

Beware of damage caused by delay. "Procrastination" means an unjustifiable excuse for not doing the job. Other than prudence, there are other factors that lead to procrastination, like doubt.

Doubt is not a bad thing, and it may be useful at times to prevent our mistakes, but it can be poisonous if it is to interfere with all of our work and overshadow our business life.

Excessive influence of doubt leads to procrastination.

I read somewhere:

- "Suspicion and doubt are the plagues of success."

A tip!

. . . You can never reach the city of success on the road of doubt. If you are really skeptical about the decision you have made, do a quick research and seek expert advice. Do not allow too much doubt overshadow your progress framework.

All people are fascinated by new ideas and designs. People want things they have not experienced before. On the other hand, 30% of the world's population have innovative ideas and plans.

When you postpone your new decision, you give an opportunity to others to overtake. Never think that the idea you have come up with is unique. No. Certainly, the new plan and ideas you have are either already known by many or are being implemented. But the real winner is the one who puts the idea into action at the earliest opportunity.

The notion that only you have the idea is a misconception.

Every day, millions of thinking brains who have ideas around the world are researching and presenting innovative plans. In this case, how is it possible that the idea that flourished in your mind could be pristine? I repeat again, the real winner is the one who decides and acts sooner.

I myself (the author of this book) am a victim of procrastination ...

It had been ten years that I had an interesting idea in the field of urban transport and traffic. I thought no one in the world would be thinking about the same idea! Therefore, I underestimated my plan and delayed to find an investor until one day my passion for the idea subsided and was extinguished! Do you know why?... Because one day when I was discussing it with an investor, the investor laughed at my elaboration of the plan and said:

- "It is going on right now in this or that city. In Dubai, too ... I would have invested if you had moved in earlier. Now, this plan has no return on investment for me anymore."

When you yourself believe in the speedy action in the world, then why delay?

One of the factors that make most people fail to achieve their goals is procrastination. An example:

Anything burnt by fire is actually destroyed. It has lost its quality and substance and no longer returns to its former state. "Procrastination" is like a fire that burns opportunities and moments. The time that is lost will never come back again.

DECISIVENESS

Your value as a manager is revealed when you make sound decisions. But when you implement a decision with complete decisiveness, you add to your credibility.

One day a salient manager took over the leadership of an almost bankrupt company. Within two days, he fired all the personnel of the company! This conclusive decision was considered a cruel decision. A wave of staff protests and disgust ensued. But what do you think was the reaction of the new manager?... In response to the repeated protests, the new manager said:

- "The staff were of no use! If they were useful, the company would not have been in this crisis!"

While the managers' harsh decisions and actions are considered ruthless and some people view the business world as a cruel one, in fact, it is not so harsh. The business world is dependent on profit and sales, and in order to achieve greater profit and for survival, it has to be governed by firm decisions.

If an organization continues to maintain its progressive structure by replacing, adjusting and layoffs toward growth and excellence, that organization is a powerful organization. Firm decisions are a strategy for survival.

Serious and decisive managers are successful and victorious managers.

A manager whose decision does not change and is persistent in his decision-making is a capable manager. Once I was scheduled to meet a powerful manager. Ironically, this decisive executive was referred to as a tyrannical autocrat. However, after meeting him I realized that what they were saying was not true at all. This decisive manager pointed out an interesting thing in his remarks:

- "...I am very determined in my decisions. Because I believe, life is short. Whatever I am going to do, I have to do it today. Many things need to be done at once. I want a lot of things too. So I go for it right now. There are many opportunities for me every day. I should not postpone these opportunities tomorrow. There may be no tomorrow for me. But unfortunately with this seriousness and decisiveness, others think I am a cruel, tyrannical, and autocrat manager. I am just serious and determined..."

A manager who lacks decisiveness has not fulfilled the management duty well. The most important task of management is making firm decisions.

If an organization gives up on "decisiveness", negative thoughts and energies replace it, leading the organization to isolation and collapse. An effective manager must either stand up to or fight against negative thoughts, or he will lose all his valuable assets.

A decisive manager always believes: ...if I do not implement my decision right now, there will be no change in my situation.

A manager who is not decisive and is accustomed to postpone today's work to tomorrow is either slave to other people's opinions or has no credibility, or he is constantly reviewing and delaying. Such a manager is heavily victimized by negative waves and will have to give up his decision.

As you know, "decisiveness" is like a fortress that prevents the absorption of negative wavelengths and malicious comments. "Decisiveness" prevents weeds to grow in the manager's mind. Weeds have never been and will never be suitable for cultivation. They are doomed to destruction.

With firm decisions, you will take a stand against any negative energies. When a man (this amazing creature) is able to get exactly what he wants, why not get it? This achievement requires firm decision-making.

Decisiveness is a highlight in the lives of successful people.

Let's not forget that "success" is more about what we are than what we have. What is the point when we have a huge factory with thousands of staff but we are not confident in our decisions? The bigger and wider your organization, the more assertive you must be.

An example:

Bicycle tires are never used for a trailer truck. The trailer truck requires its own massive and solid tires. It is your decisiveness that, like massive tires, will have the power to carry on and control a large organization.

THE PLAN, A MUST

The fact is that the public does not have a plan to live a good life and a successful business as much as it plans for a holiday. Jim Ran says this to confirm this fact:
- *"Probably because it is easier to escape reality than to accept change!"*

We have to plan for all moments of our lives. If we are not a good planner, we have to obey others' planning. Certainly, other people's plans are designed solely to fulfill their goals, not our goals. It is here that we become enslaved to others.

Proper planning is like an instruction that tells us the beginning and the end of the work. Someone who has planned for the next days, weeks, and months will continue to do his job joyfully and energetically. However, the reason many people are frightened of the future is that they are "unplanned". When planning matters so much, why should not a manager use it in his administrative affairs?

Planning is a requirement in the field of management. The manager whose one-year plan has been formulated manages the current matters with ease. A consistent work plan defines the density and scope of work for us. It is at this time that we can master the details.

With the right plan, you are going to reduce the clutter, although you run a large organization and you are very busy. The more comfortable you are; the better you will handle the matters. Thomas Edison has an interesting statement:

- "Being too busy does not always mean real work. The point of doing all of the work means productivity and success. The appearance of being at work is beating around the bush."

A "good plan" is a high-quality plan.

One of the most prominent of these qualities is the alignment of the plan with your goals. It should be planned in a way to achieve goals faster, more comprehensively and more calculated. James McTillow, author of *Time Management at Work and Life*, writes:

- *"It is very important to make a connection between life goals and daily tasks. A manager should not plan to do trivial and low-yield tasks."*

A great manager thinks of big goals and plans to achieve them. Basically, the nature of planning is toward growth and excellence. What planning does a person who does not think about growth and excellence and success might have? This person just plans for sleeping, amusement, eating and drinking. Good planning is useful when you think about maximum and more productivity. Planning helps, you achieve your goals without wasting time. Professional management needs these things.

If your plans improve every day relative to the previous days, then planning is valuable. Many people set goals, believe in those goals, decide to act, but do not think they need to plan before action.

An organization without a plan is a clueless organization (its purpose is lost like a needle in a haystack).

The first thing "the plan" asks from a manager is his ultimate goal. One of the pillars of planning is the listing of actions. Make a list of your tasks, prioritize them, and include them in your planning.

If you own a huge organization, you should be more of a planner. Because a big organization has big goals. Any great work will go ahead with ease through planning.

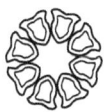

CREATING A FOUNDATION

The strength of a building depends on its foundation. A work plan needs both a daily list and a weekly list. Now that you are reading this text, you need to know what your plan is for tomorrow, the next week, and the next month.

Knowing what to do the next day will make you orderly. You need to know that you have an important role to play in changing the quality of your tomorrow. If you believe this important role well, you will be a planner. The concern of a successful and planning manager is:

- Tomorrow I am going to do this ...

- The day after tomorrow I am going to do that ...

A more successful manager has a different and better plan every day relative to previous days. Where there is a list, shortcomings no longer exist. Because the "list" is an infinite capacity. You can incorporate whatever you want into your list and strengthen your planning foundation to achieve your goals strongly.

A plan needs boundaries and frameworks that are set by the size of your business. Besides the list, prioritizing is another part of the foundation, that is, which task is important and which one is not important.

I do not know that for you, who are reading this text right now, what is important and what is not important. Our recommendation is to prioritize topics that are more productive, effective or get you to your goals sooner than usual. One day I asked a manager about his schedule, list, and priorities, and he answered:

- "Without a plan, I cannot run my factory. I have listed all of these plans and our priority is to keep the staff satisfied. All I have is my staff. What plans would I have without them? What list can I write? I believe keeping staff happy affects product quality consistency and this same consistency of quality equals customer satisfaction."

Everyone has a priority for their work. What is your priority? The top priority of a CEO was to enter the stock market... other managers have other top priorities like customer satisfaction... setting up a staff training workshop... to keep current conditions... to patent a new idea for the company ... to launch the production line for a certain part and cutting on dependency to outside... transfer of a part of shares and so on.

You know better what you want and what you have in mind. It is important that your plan has a clear and prioritized list. With an irregular list, you cannot get things done. That is called carelessness!

A manager may also be careless! Many executives resort to excuses such as too many things to so and heavy responsibility to justify their carelessness. But, as we mentioned earlier, you can tidy things up by planning (no matter how large your organization is).

Lack of planning has a clear origin and that is the lack of clear purpose. Naturally, when there is a specific goal, a specific plan will follow. If there is a plan, laying the foundation will follow.

Nowhere in the world has anyone been able to get anywhere unless he has a predefined plan. Goal and success are not like things that you sit at home and someone arrives to give them to you in a gift-wrap. The goal and success require planning. The plan itself also needs a foundation and an index.

All of these steps are achieved with passion, interest, and desire for success, throw in some diligence that seems so essential. Remember a statement by Bill Gates (the richest man in the world for many consecutive years):

- "Many people like to be in my place! But none of those people are willing to go through the ordeals I have experienced."

ORGANIZING

When you have a plan for your work and consequently a list, think about organizing.

Organize your schedule for every week, month, and year. Organizing means checking whether the things that should be at their place are there or not. Crises, economic struggles, and sudden failures are foreseeable and these disasters can destroy all your plans. We said earlier that the situation is not always going to be in your favor.

You may be able to determine the internal conditions of your organization and do things very strongly, but what impact do you have on the external conditions? How much do you influence the market situation and competitors' qualitative conditions?

Therefore, since your impact on the external economy and market is not a hundred percent, then you ought to take into account the possibility of a major economic hurricane. Match your plans with the daily quality of economics to get rid of bad conditions. The purpose of organizing is to match the plans with the economy of the day. You cannot plan for something that tomorrow's economy and the market will reject. The reason for the failure of some companies is the lack of a comprehensive plan and a new idea for tomorrow's.

Disorderly plans will not bring you the profit and efficiency you need. "Organizing" and adapting to the present day is not about giving up on ideas innovation, it means considering external conditions and accepting some facts.

Some of your activities that were already included in your plans and could have been effective) will no longer work (as the current conditions change). Discard them now and do not tie your mind to them forever. Since humanity is advancing at breakneck speed, you cannot afford a disorderly plan. If you have a long-term plan, include tomorrow's changing conditions in it. Short-term plans allow you to incorporate new strategies into them.

If you have written a five-year plan, keep the door open for innovative and diverse ideas within it. You cannot devise a rigid plan written in stone that does not accept change for your next five years, because the conditions are not always the same.

None of your managers can sign a five-year unyielding plan. Because you have come to realize that if you are not going to change for five years, you will perish. "Organizing," tells you:

- "Constantly check and review the plans and lists. Remove some extras and add some new plans."

In the future, we will tell you what are the benefits or disadvantages of changing the plans.

Change of the plans is good, but not always useful. We will elaborate on this matter for you. At present, think about organizing your plans.

If you change a "plan", it should be based on a comprehensive, up-to-date and innovative strategy. Otherwise, constantly changing plans will seriously damage your administrative system. The new plan should include a new idea that no one ever came up with or few have thought of it.

It is the exquisite idea that renders the plan innovative.

A great manager is thinking about growth for success. He thinks about the idea. He thinks about things that drive both the people around him and the community toward progress. The plans of a successful manager are generally organized. Everything is in order and interesting ideas are added to them depending on the daily conditions (perhaps even ahead of the present time). This is not a change but an evolution.

Just as the appearance of a person, his intrinsic moods, behavior, wardrobe, desk, work office, and living space need to be refined and organized, the plan is no different. Instead of constantly changing plans, think about organizing plans.

The staff like this method more. Many things disturb your plans. Dealing with disturbances is an important part of a manager's job.

Dealing with disturbances and interruptions is part of organizing the plans. (A quote from James McTillow): '*On average, managers get interrupted and disturbed every six minutes*'.

Therefore, we insist that you must continuously keep track of your plans. Any manager, who cannot check his plans, will not bring them to fruition. How is it possible that a gardener does not check on his garden for a day? The presence of the gardener in the garden is as important as oxygen and water for the tree. The gardener irrigates by digging a creek. He eradicates the weeds and sometimes prunes the trees, and sometimes plants seedlings. This means organizing.

It is very important to have a gardener sorting out a garden. You are the gardener of your plans. Organize them every day and every day.

BRIEF AND HELPFUL

There are large companies and organizations that have extensive plans, but sometimes get sickan d lose their performance due to clutter and false complexity, as well as inattentiveness.

Interestingly, some executives consider so much confusion and complexity as the vision of their organization! If indeed the vision is defined by complex and ambiguous plans, it is hardly possible for them to achieve their goals.

Since the plan is absolutely necessary, it should be simple, comprehensible and achievable. Simplicity and brevity of the plan do not mean it is trivial. Many a simple plan is there in the world that has led to huge changes in an organization.

That is why they say 'great promise, small performance'. If an executive shows you a huge scroll of his plans (which even ten trailer trucks cannot carry), you can be sure that %60 of that scroll contains a pile of pipe dreams and fantasies.

The mountain can be moved when you start by removing pebbles from the foot of the mountain. Having a plan is important, but do not doubt that it is not as important as having a concise and useful plan. Once an engineer was hired by a company. After signing the engineer's appointment letter, the CEO asked:

- "I need to know your plans!"

The newly hired engineer started for an hour describing goals, plans, work strategies, and prospects! The CEO said with total frustration:

- "Stop it, sir! At present, your plan is to arrive on time for work tomorrow. Just that."

It is not right to be caught up in the labyrinth of large-scale plans. Start by implementing small and concise plans and move on systematically. Usain Bolt (one of the fastest men in the world at two-hundred-meter races) was a kid who could not stand on his two legs and like all the kids in the world learnt walking by continuous falling; otherwise, he was not born a world champion.

Empower yourself to manage big and large-scale plans by implementing small plans. How can a person who is unable not do a small job handle big plans?

Summarize your plans in a few paragraphs and check them with your organization's trustworthy staff. The more concise a plan is, the more comprehensible it will be. Elaborate plans require a great deal of organizing. Once at a seminar, I asked a great executive about his plans. On a piece of paper, he wrote me his plans in six paragraphs. I asked with surprise:

- "You have a large corporation, and then your plans boil down to six paragraphs?"

The CEO replied with high confidence:

- "Our plans are brief on paper but complete in practice."

Summarizing a plan is divided into three categories:

- Plan title
- Execution agents
- Execution date

Here are some of the key features of successful people:

They never leave home without a plan. Each plan is complementary to its previous one. They have a list of their plans. Simple and accessible items are their top priority. They do not go to the second one until they have completed the first one. The arrangement of their plans is merely for a specific purpose. They use past experience to make their plans more mature. Their plans are concise and useful.

However, what matters most to successful people is "having a plan". Set a goal for yourself to have a specific vision. With having a "plan", this task takes on a practical aspect. Afterward, review your plans and write a summary of the most important ones.

These important plans, although small and concise, are useful and will benefit you and your future career.

MARGINAL FUNCTIONS

It is not unthinkable that a predefined plan might occasionally get caught up in marginal and deterrent events. If all the plans were to succeed, everyone could have achieved their goals without any hassle, and then "endurance", "pursuit" and "gaining experience" would have no meaning.

So the existence of margins, barriers and deterrents are natural. The reason they say success does not come overnight and you have to pay a price for it is these hurdles and obstacles ahead. In order to succeed, you have to bear the margins and obstacles. In fact, any margin is an obstacle because it is a deterrent factor.

The speed and plans of a manager trapped in marginal functions are slowed down subconsciously. They never compare the speed of a one-hundred-meter runner with a steeplechase runner. If planning has a definite pathway and there is a purpose behind it, addressing the margins will throw you into the hole of indecisiveness.

What most confuses the manager on the margin is the negative wavelengths and energies of the failed and outcast people. The same people whose lives ended with a single failure, and with harmful words and attitudes like 'I know it will not work', they block the execution of other people's plans.

Carefully choose your friends, companions, and advisors to get rid of such energy vampires. Someone who is not willing that a purposeful person with a plan gets results will throw in a thousand reasons and buts & ifs to make him deviate from his path. These margins are dangerous and we warn you right now to get more alert.

An example: ... Do you know any driver who drives without a windshield wiper on a rainy day? Clearly, the rain will not allow the driver to see and drive.

You must have a wiper for your "planning" steps and leaps. Because you have to always assume that the business climate is cloudy. This assumption is a valid assumption. The business climate is teeming with failed and isolated people with ceaseless negative precipitation. Be careful. You need to know what conditions you live in.

What is the wiper of your plans? Having "faith in work" is the best windshield wiper of negative precipitation. It is natural that if you believe your plans will work, it is much more effective than the actions carried out with doubt and procrastination, continuously manipulated by other people's negative wavelengths and sidetracking.

Faith in the realization of plans leads to perseverance and diligence. Any plan supported with perseverance and diligence will definitely work.

I knew an executive whose planning strategy was based on counsel. When I talked to him about "work margins", he made an interesting point:

- "All our lives are caught up in margins. But I will not allow myself to get sidetracked. All the people I consult with are successful and self-made persons who point out the dangers of sidetracking, not the kind of people who themselves are deeply into sidetracking to their eyeballs . . .

John C. Maxwell writes in the book, *Making of Oneself*:

- "*. . . all those whose dreams came true were dedicated to the process of work.*"

It is natural for all people to tend toward stagnation, weakness, and margins, but staying in a state of stagnation, weakness, and margins will destroy you. Failure is okay because the only way for you to succeed is to fail first, fail repeatedly, and direct your failures toward success.

Since the margins are always there, it is okay to deal with them and bypass them, but it is a disaster to stay in their swamp. Clever and wise people both learn from dealing with margins and benefit from it. However, the wretched people become a slave to the margins and their miserable lives.

The wretched people are the real captives of the margins. Those ones will be oblivious of good and high-class life forever.

DISCIPLINE

"Discipline" is the most critical part of planning. Clearly, "order" is the most important element in the business world, and maintaining order is part of the important tasks in the world of executives. Simply put, everything has to be in place, and every plan needs to be organized systematically.

When you implement any plan in a defined and specific situation, it means your plan is orderly.

When you appoint the responsibility of an agent (according to his expertise and ability) to execute the plan, your plans are regulated. You can work better with three capable people (who are very well versed in their responsibilities) and advance the plans than a hundred people, none of which are at the place they deserve.

Every organization and company has its own plans, but it is interesting to note that most of these plans are not arranged according to work order. If the components of a mechanical engine are not neatly and securely in place, the engine will fail. It is a fact. So is the organization in the business world. See your organization from this perspective. An organization is no different from a mechanical engine. It needs both technical inspection and repair! Maintenance also has its place.

There will be always numerous rewards for a disciplined effort. How systematic are you in your work? If you have a specific plan and goal, you must not forget that achieving goals requires a great deal of work discipline. The business world has proven that no one will succeed with negligence, laziness, and lack of planning.

Negligence and indiscipline have a negative impact on the work process. Just like rotten apples that ruin the rest of the apples in the box. "Indiscipline" overshadows all parts of the organization and leads to organizational chaos.

"Planning", "identifying and removing margins", "follow up on practical measures". These three elements will help you a lot to keep your plans in order. John Edder writes in the book, *Creative Thinking Skills*:

- "*. . . planning means building a mental bridge between where you are now and where you want to be.*"

You definitely need work discipline, personal discipline, and execution discipline. You cross the river by jumping on several rocks. Doing so in an orderly manner will result in you crossing the river, otherwise, with your disorderly jumps, you will inevitably fall into the river.

For a well-ordered person, it is very easy to do complicated and hard tasks. If your organizational structure is disciplined and orderly, you have added to your attractiveness in the business world.

It is natural that anyone seeing a tidy child will first admire the child's parents. When you are at the top of your organizational affairs, you should be aware that your organization is in the focus of critics and public opinion as your child. When an orderly system is in place in your organization, the subconscious minds of others are directed toward the management and salute it. Whether the manager is firm and rigid or soft and flexible. The important thing is the thousands of salutes pouring in for him. Each case of admiration strengthens your customers' market.

"Discipline" is directly in the public view. From the perspective of customers in the business market, the quality and price of many organizations and companies are measured by discipline. So one cannot simply overlook the "discipline".

IDEA AND PLAN

A plan gets its value from its attractiveness, otherwise old and regular plans and plans lacking a new idea are not worth spending time on them. It is true that having a plan is good, but having a good plan is different.

A white piece of paper, no matter how smooth, clean, and glossy, will not worth putting in a frame unless it has a good image and text. A plan must have a strategy. The distinction between a painting canvas and a drawing canvas is in color. So it could be more expensive.

Decorate your plans with exquisite and pristine designs to make them more expensive. No one can say firmly that I have such a plan, while he has not specified any new strategy for it. Certainly, his plans were no more than fantasies. A plan must have a blueprint, a final version, designed and developed perfectly. Only in this case, one may claim there is a plan.

An organization needs to consider new and sophisticated ideas for planning to avoid falling into the pit of daily routine and stagnation. Let us not forget that with the old and burned out plans of the previous years, one cannot hope for success. Your plans should be reviewed every now and then. New ideas (which lead to progress of the work) should be used in plans.

It is these ideas that eventually become the plan because the ideas are born from a rich mind. When we want to execute a plan, we need to convert it to an execution plan. All inventors and innovators (before planning) have weighed many ideas in their minds so that they could write a plan for them.

Remember to throw away our old and burnt out plans and forge new and innovative ideas. This is the main strategy of change. If we do not change, we are doomed to destruction. The only way out of bankruptcy in the business world is to keep up-to-date and stay up-to-date. Keep on planning to advance. Thousands of ideas can be evoked in mind, but the plan must be implemented.

The idea changes hundreds of times, but these changes occur less frequently in a plan. You are free to create innovative ideas for whatever drives your organization toward growth and progress, and when these ideas are hammered out; your plans will be aligned.

You may have heard that many managers are constantly changing their plans! This constant change leads to stagnation. They pretend that they are constantly updating and innovating, unaware that it entraps the staff in an awful mess called "confusion".

The staff wants their fate to be clear for a long time, rather than be a plaything of the manager's volatile strategies and plans every day. The idea may change, but the successive change of plans discourages and kills the incentive in staff. That is why we emphasize that an organization must have a vision, and plan accordingly.

I have had meetings with a lot of corporate and administrative staff. I understood some important points in these conversations. One of the things I noticed was that most of the staff were not willing to work! Frustration and disappointment could be seen in their behavior and speech. Much unhappy staff has this to say:

- "...We have a manager without a plan! It is not clear what it does! Even when he has plans, he changes them regularly! We do not know to dance to which of his tunes! So, we do not care about the manager's progress or the manager's downfall! We work just to get a fistful of dollars!"

The personnel, although they do not play a role in the manager's organizational plans, they notice the ideas and plans well and understand it well. Because they work under the same managerial ideas and plans every day, engaging with them in every moment. Because their responsibilities are distributed according to the idea and plan. therefore, we must implement the structure of the plan with a broad and progressive vision, so as to ensure the firm's long-term viability and survival and do not suffer drastic and damaging changes.

One key point:
As a manager, what do you think about "flying" and "throwing"? (Think a little bit) . . . Naturally, most people think of "throwing". To be thrown by others into a world of success and prosperity and a world of power and wealth. But great people and top executives do not think about "throwing", they think of "flying." To fly to the world of success and prosperity with effort and perseverance.

In the "throw", you do not decide but others decide for you. While it is not so in "flight". Thus, the "throw" radius is far less than the "flight" radius. Think about flying before you are thrown to where others want.

Notes:

No one can claim to have the power to remember things (without failure). One should doubt the sanity of a person who trusts in his memory. How on earth the memory could be trusted?

Undoubtedly, the "memory" has the power to preserve some matters. But what about all of them? Is the manager so free and idle to spend time keeping ideas and plans in mind?

So, we find that memory, although important, is less efficient in the field of management. Many managers make promises and go under many commitments but carry out none! Do you know why? Because they had kept those promises and commitments in memory instead of putting them down!

Human beings are inherently forgetful. Given this fact, why should we trust the memory and entrust it with carrying out the matters? Carrying out matters and schedules are only possible by taking notes and recording. Ideas, strategies, and plans have complexities that no matter how powerful the memory is, it still cannot remember all. The best place to record ideas, plans and information is the notebook, not the memory. Even the smartest managers take notes of their daily routine.

A true story:

... One day, with a group of friends we went to visit the late *Allama Mohammad Taghi Jafari*. After a few minutes of speech, he asked us all:

- "Did you understand anything I said?"

We all said in unison:

- "Yes !!"

The sage laughed and said:

- "I take God as a witness you did not understand anything! Because none of you were writing down what I was saying! You just memorized my words and tomorrow you forget all that!"

(The sage was right. After years of visiting that place, I still do not remember what he was saying!)

Somewhere I read:

- "There are three things you can leave behind. Your photos, your library, and your personal notes."

For your future generations, these three things will be much more valuable than home furniture. The more uncrowded the mind and memory are, the easier it is to analyze things and find the right solutions. I repeat: . . . the place of plans and ideas in not in the memory, it is in the notebook.

What great scientists that have come and gone throughout history and the writings they left behind. These valuable writings are now of great value to science researchers. You cannot convey your mind's reserves to future generations unless you write and keep all of them.

Do you know if you are not good at taking notes you miss many lessons and tips during a day?

Now that you are reading this text, how many key points have you received and put down? Rest assured, after reading these texts today, tomorrow and other tomorrows, you will not remember any of these words and texts. This is not deliberate forgetfulness! It is human nature.

The only way to get rid of forgetfulness is "to take notes".

Taking notes of key points and ideas is not a spelling exercise or a homework assignment, but rather the preservation of the most valuable things that will be useful someday. If you see someone who writes down his daily affairs and writes down tomorrow's plans, that person is not out of memory or stupid. Incidentally, he is very smart and thoughtful. Someone who does not trust his memory and this is the best thing for a progressive man.

All the small or big management matters are embedded in a seemingly insignificant thing called "taking notes."

A question:

Why do you think the handwriting of deceased celebrities in the world's biggest auctions have such high price offers? Prices far above a fine painting?

At many research centers and universities, there is still extensive research on the writings of past scientists. All around us are full of ideas that need to be taken note of and used.

Therefore, one always must have a pen at hand. Since some notes were taken at present (that cannot be used today), someday they will be useful. Imagine a day that to solve a problem you have to leaf through past writings and at that time, the memory will not come to your help. And the last word . . .

- "Never start your day unless you have already finished it on paper."

WORK LESSON

What is the "work lesson"? The work lesson is a set of experiences at work. All successful people in the world recognize that their failures in the business world not only did not push them back but also taught them many lessons to learn from those failures.

When a simple workplace or a large work environment is full of different doctrines, it means that working makes people more mature and that work environment is a comprehensive practical university. If there is learning science in universities, there is also learning experience in the workplace.

When science and experience are combined, it will be easier to achieve the goals and wishes.

But let's see which one of the experience or science works best.

Experience is a valuable practical product, but science is a valuable impractical product. How different is it to see an object, hear about it, and even touch it? Science talks to you about some things, but experience engages you with some matters.

You will not reap benefits until your efforts and information are blended with the practical experience of that knowledge and information. Gaining experience and learning work are very valuable.

There is a unique and limited framework for science, while there lies mysterious and vast world inexperience. To succeed, you have to get yourself involved in the job and fail repeatedly. It is in the world of work that failures are tangible and you really learn the lesson.

Where in science does "failure" really makes sense? No matter how much you want to explain a topic, the people will not be convinced unless you understand and touch it at close quarters. The workplace is a great learning environment. Managers need to know that only a few things can be done with "pen and knowledge" but much more can be done with "experience".

"Experience" is embedded inside the work and "experience" familiarizes you with the world of mistakes. An English proverb:

"The one who does nothing wrong does not right either."

Gaining experience in business teaches us to move forward despite mistakes. The mistakes are automatically forgotten. These basic and precious teachings are not found in any prominent universities. Although topics are saved and preserved well at the science centers, they do not include how to overcome obstacles and problems. If your plan were built upon your experience, you would achieve your goals better.

The reason many educated people who enter the business world are frustrated is that they lack experience. This is not an easy matter. This involves a great number of graduates.

One should not expect to succeed in the sophisticated business world just by having the highest academic certificates. But sometimes "experience" has led many illiterate people to success.

The opportunity to learn in difficult situations is provided by overcoming mistakes. These kinds of mistakes are good! As they, lead you to make your planning more complete and to arrange the execution puzzle of matters correctly. Thomas Edison was truly a master of experience. When the prodigy's lab burned to the ground and turned to ashes, he said:

- "Thank God! All my mistakes burned! Now I can start again!"

The experience constantly forces you to start over again. This constant renewal is the comprehensive doctrine of the work lesson. John C. Maxwell states in his book Failure, the Beginning of Victory:

- "Starting anew is usually not easy. At least it is easy to say. But no doubt the results are astonishing."

A successful manager is always in search of learning, and that learning lies in a world of mistakes and failures. Basically, the world of business and experience is not comparable with that of science. Each one has its own characteristics.

A manager should not assume that he knows everything by having the highest scientific certificate. He will not realize his grade unless he enters the arena and certainly, he will go nowhere.

CONFORMANCE BETWEEN GOAL AND PLAN

The two main pillars of a successful business are goals and plans. These two principles are interdependent. That is to say, there is no meaning to the plan unless there is a goal, and no goal is achieved unless there is a plan.

The "goal" is the endpoint and the "plan" is how to reach the endpoint. So they can never be separated. Getting to the goal early or late depends on the quality of the plan.

A quality plan makes the "goal" more accessible and a poor quality plan makes the "goal" intangible. Before dreaming about your goals, see what your plan looks like. See how well your plan can be implemented?

A quality plan is a plan that has elements such as passion, motivation, action, perseverance, stamina and the like. Because the goal will not be achieved easily. Expect a variety of issues and obstacles when you set out on a specific goal. If these plans are simple and ordinary, you will definitely have to redirect, retreat and start again. While a high-quality plan lets you easily, overcome problems and obstacles. A quality plan indicates that, for example, in these circumstances, that thing must be done, or a certain experience should be used in the face of a certain crisis.

Remember, "Goal quality" does not matter at all, but the "plan quality" is important. It is not the goal that should be solid, but the plan should be solid. No one cares about the looks and colors of the target or where it is located but cares about with what bow you are pointing at it and what your viewing angle is.

The main factor in evaluating an archer is his precision and targeting style, not the target that he has to hit. You need to have a calculated plan to reach your goal.

A hurried plan, a complex plan, and a confused plan with poor quality is not worth pursuing. Do not waste your time. Review the nature and quality of your plan. In a "comprehensive plan" to achieve the goal, there must be a passion and a desire to achieve the goal with the necessary motivation and inner urge. The important thing is not to reach the goal early; it is to reach the goal *per se*.

At a world running competition, after the champion and other runners crossed the finish line and were awarded prizes, when spectators were leaving the stadium, suddenly a lame runner who was left behind approached the finish line and caught everyone's attention. The lame runner crossed the finish line in front of the stunned spectators and sat on the ground panting heavily! The spectators began to cheer despite the race was over. A few reporters gathered around the lame runner. A reporter asked:

- "Why did you keep going despite being the last one?"

The runner said breathlessly:

- "I had promised the people of my country to cross the finish line. It does not matter if I am not the first one! The important thing is I finally reached it!"

Reaching the goal is much more important than being early or late. Speeding up a plan is not a feat. Upgrading the plan is a feat.

Many people who fail to achieve their goals are trapped in a number of factors. Either they are in a hurry! Or they (by focusing on the margins) are sidetracked, or their schedules are too crowded and carelessly devised.

The biggest puzzle in the world of managers is not choosing the type of goal; it is choosing a plan to achieve the goal. How to go, when to go, and how to deal with challenges. Failure and frustration are due to the lack of skill in solving such puzzles. Of course, failure and frustration are not bad. They seem very necessary because they increase your ability to solve success puzzles. These puzzles are hidden between the layers of your plans.

CONFORMANCE OF GOAL AND PLAN
(Another look)

Management deals with two things and its life are tied to those two things. One is the goal and the other, the plan. Dealing with the goal makes the person purposeful, and dealing with the plan makes one disciplined and a planner.

There are many managers who are purposeful but never achieve their goals! This failure has one reason, and that is the disordered plan. But a disciplined manager with a plan will certainly achieve his goals.

Therefore, we find that planning is much more effective than having a goal. Many people in the community have no goal and want to achieve many things! (Moreover, they think about flourishing!) What percentage of these people do you think are successful?

Many of these people stop at their first failure. However, these failures are very necessary to make them mature. Simply having a goal is not a success. Having the right plan and executing it correctly is a success.

This is why they say: 'a guy with a plan will certainly succeed'.

During planning, you will encounter dead ends, some of which are so difficult to deter you from progress. In fact, these dead ends teach people the art of opening a pathway and removing them.

The path to success is not paved well so that you can move fast in it. A rational and logical plan is a plan that predicts the obstacles, and in fact, it is a solution *per se*. A plan that includes ways out of crises and challenges is a strategic and sound plan that is worth pursuing. Sound plans can be regarded as a valuable resource for a successful manager. Such plans are expensive. Like valuable artworks, some of which cannot even be priced.

Getting to the goal is no different than conquering a mountain peak. Do you know a mountain without highs and lows? If it does not have peaks and valleys, can it be called a mountain? A climber starts out with a pre-defined plan. The taller and more difficult climbing a mountain is, the more accurate is the climber's plan and more extensive his training will be. Once, an Iranian climber who has conquered many mountain peaks in Iran and around the world told me:

- "I have been in the team's training camp for a month. These exercises will take a year."

When I asked the reason for this long exercise, he replied:

- "We are getting ready to climb to the K2 summit, which is about the same size as Everest and the second tallest peak in the world . . . It is also the toughest mountain in the world. With deep valleys and dangerous walls. We, who have conquered some of the world's tallest peaks and have even more climbing experience, are still training one year for the big goal."

Do not think the "big goal" will be achieved overnight.

Management Clinic

A great and worthwhile goal should have systematic and valuable planning. Do not go for big goals with everyday boring plans, or with small and worthless plans. It is a large and disciplined plan that can achieve your goals quickly.

In a mountaineering camp with 1000 strong for conquering Everest peak, why only two hundred people reach 5,000 meters, one hundred people 6,000 meters, fifty people 7,000 meters, and ten people 8,000 meters? And why do only three to four people succeed in conquering the summit?

Powerful, experienced and purposeful people are the main conquerors of success peaks. To reach the goal, smart (but less experienced) people learn from experienced people. This is the best thing in the world of success. Climbers move toward the summit in succession (in terms of experience and skill). Less experienced climbers in the middle and end of the queue should pay attention to two important points. One is: follow the footsteps of more experienced people, and two: never leave the team and walk individually. The hardheaded, lawless, or separatist climbers either do not reach the summit or, if they do, will arrive too late with much difficulty.

Clearly, not obeying more climbers that are experienced will cause trouble for them. These two important rules are widely used in the business world.

Experienced people are your best advisors for reaching your goals. They have good plans and will show you the right paths. Do not be afraid of the height and bumpy path of the mountain when you have experienced consultants and successful friends around you. Move on and up like an eagle just thinking about climbing. The eagles live at heights unlike ducks in the mud and swamp. If you stand down below, the summit will not bend toward you. Do not forget this. Put down this good statement as the final sentence of this topic somewhere:

- "From the bottom of the valley, the peak seems too high."

More interestingly: ... the paved road is for the lowlands, not the steep mountains. The asphalt-paved road is a smooth road for the public and belongs to everyone, but certain people travel along steep, bumpy and difficult roads.

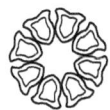

TIME

We all believe that there are many surprises in the world while not paying attention to a wonder of the universe, e.g. "time". More interestingly, each of us humans (collectively and equally) has 24 hours a day at his disposal.

Everyone uses these 24 hours a day depending on his plans and tasks. The 24 hours includes 3 eight hours. Eight hours of sleep, 8 hours of work, and 8 hours for the rest. The question is what happens in this remaining 8 hours of our time?

With a brief calculation, we find out what hours we waste during the day. "Time" is a gift that is irrevocable. If we say, "time" is a big wonder it is because of these three elements:

- No one knows the future and its quality and characteristics
- It shows its best productivity now and at present
- When it is gone, it will not come back

Realizing these three principles, we realize the importance and value of time. We find out what valuable asset we have.

90% of mature and wise people in the world believe:

- "... I wish I could turn back time to compensate for the opportunities I have missed in vain!"

The remaining %10 of those people do not say that! They know the value of time and use it in the best possible way. In what category are you, who are reading this book? %90 or %10?

"Time" is the most valuable asset of a human being.

Willy-nilly, everyone has a price for his time. Some trade 8 hours of it for a conventional salary. Some sell 10 hours of it, and some (excluding 10 hours of sleep) spend the remaining 14 hours of it idling away, eventually joining the mass %90 of the population.

Some also work many hours around the clock (more than the labor law's stipulation) for a few dollars more! On the other hand, there are some people who are making the most of their time. "Days" and "nights" are our real assets. Because they have the precious gem of the time.

When a day is wasted, a great deal of capital is toast.

The real capitalist is the one who makes the most of his days and times. Wealth is also valuable, but not as much as time. Because wealth can be gained but not lost time. The one who makes the most of his time has in fact transformed himself from being "active" to "being effective".

Before you think about being active, think about being effective. Many people like to be influenced by you rather than see you die by hard work. One may not imagine anything more valuable than time, but many great people think there is something more valuable than time! More valuable than time is people who have realized the value of time and are making good use of it.

Management Clinic

We are faced with a set of tasks and options every day. If we cannot distinguish essentials from unnecessary things, we have lost our precious "time". Because the best way to use time is to deal with the necessities of life rather than the unnecessary and life-wasting matters.

In the field of management, managers often fail to identify and distinguish important matters. While time management is more necessary than managing matters. Matters are always there and current, but what about time?. . Time may not be available tomorrow. Richard H. Nixon says:

- "Never allow "Yesterday" to consume the "Today" portion."

Make the most of every day's quality and opportunity and get ready to exploit tomorrow's quality. Today's work should be done today and not postponed to tomorrow and tomorrow.

WORKING HOURS

"Working hours" is a specific time frame for doing things and the staff receive their salaries according to it. For the staff, "working hours" are even more important than how they work. So, at the beginning of employment, they ask about the working hours and when they finish work, they line up at the clock punch machine!

Our discussion is not about the quantity and quality of working hours, but about something else, we describe later. We are addressing you, dear managers, your employers, and business owners. A manager who believes he has to get up in the morning and just think about work until night and work to death! Is afflicted with unnecessary excesses in his field of management. On the other hand, a manager with dispersed and irregular working hours will also experience time instability.

Having a specific working time will allow you to come up with a good definition of time and arrange everything according to time. You need to have a specific working hour for your day.

By setting these specific working hours, you have taken the first step of work discipline and have sorted out your situation with yourself and those around you and your family.

(No matter what an overcrowded and high-ranking manager you are.)

Some managers have the advantage of more profit by staying longer and working harder because they own their business. Heavy and compressed working hours have their own definitions. Intensive working hours can lead to many physical injuries.

A person is not going to benefit by working harder. He is going to benefit from working properly. What drives the manager to have more working hours is the increase in useful work. That is to say, they think the more they work the more returns they earn. This is a misconception.

If the "benefit" lies in doing useful and effective work, you can do it in 8 hours rather than looking for it across 20 hours of intensive work. For the sake of more profit, try to increase the amount of useful work and efficiency in the same eight hours of normal organizational work. Because at this specific time, you have a set of human resources and personnel and your personal ability is multiplied by several individual capabilities.

What is the benefit of having 20 hours of your daily work and only 1 hour of effective work? So what did you do in those 19 hours?

A strong manager within a given work timeframe is looking for quality work, not quantity work. Effective useful work is not a regular, simple, and repetitive routine. Effective work is a work that is full of new designs and ideas and innovations that make good things happen.

Management Clinic

From a managerial point of view, setting working hours means setting a specific time for doing useful and profitable things. Not just presence, coming, and going. Most thinks the person only of quantitative presence rather than qualitative presence. The manager needs to think about how to improve the quality of working hours for his organization to grow. He must know that the actual energy of the staff lies within given working hours, and as soon as the end of the working day approaches, the staff's eyes are fixed at the hands of the clock and consequently, human energy also diminishes.

Efficiency does not increase by keeping the staff longer, however, disenchantment increases. The art of management (to increase staff efficiency) is revealed in specified working hours. Suppose each of the staff during the daytime and at the same specified working hours is assigned with an important part of the job. How much do you think you would have done useful work if you had more people (of the same quality)?

Distribute important and useful tasks among your staff within a given hour to see them grow.

The best way to increase the staff work quality (at specified hours) is to divide responsibilities based on ability, individual talent, commitment, and interest, otherwise, confusion over division of responsibilities reduces staff performance. Result:

... the manager's focus on the correct use of the working hours is more important than the marginal matters relating to the working hours.

TIME MANAGEMENT

Somewhere I read: "Doing everything right."
A manager does the job properly. "Doing everything right" is a broad concept with a variety of conditions. The best way to manage things is to make the most of your time. Because valuable opportunities are found only in "time" and not elsewhere. Things can be managed better with control of time.

Things are always disrupted by the slippage of time and lose their effectiveness. So, time control, in turn, needs to be addressed, which we call "time management". Time must be categorized with a specific metabolism, and its useful and useless aspects must be extracted. Over 80% of people in the community are more skilled at burning and selling their time free rather than managing it. If everyone knew how to use their time, the statistics of 80% of failed people would not be 80%.

Put a price tag on your time. This pricing also increases your price. Check how much social popularity the people in the community have? This popularity is a small fraction of their price. The world today is moving toward a perspective that prices a few things that may not have been of much value in the past. Like thought, time, health, and pristine ideas.

As a manager, you cannot manage properly if you do not have time management. Every plan (before execution) mostly needs a time schedule to do it, rather than how to do it. Always the question: 'When and at what time?' is more important than the question: 'How much and how?' This is because time's volatility is high. The time to execute your best plan may be over in an instant. Time management asks, from you dear manager, a few basic things that it does not ask from an ordinary person.

Do not postpone today's work to tomorrow since there may be no tomorrow. Go on to execute whatever new plans you have so that others will not overtake you.

Increase your time quality with useful work. Basically, a manager with a specific and executable plan can control the time. A clear and executable plan can also help you evaluate and prioritize your daily tasks. One of the most successful managers has this to say on time management:

- "Collect and record all matters, whether urgent or non-urgent, large or small, personal or general, whose completion requires serious action on your part."

"PARETO PRINCIPLE"

The Pareto Principle says: 80% of the results we get are just the result of 20% of our efforts.

In other words, %80 of our efforts will only produce %20 of our results. To go beyond this law, we must not only focus our efforts on high-return work but also ensure that our precious time is not spent on trivial and low-return work.

Always remember the 20 - 80 principle in time management. In time management, make your next actions smaller and more manageable. The smallness of any action is not a measure of its low quality. Shredding the actions and sorting them out in detail reinforces the feeling in you that you have spent a useful and productive day. Your management will allow you to eliminate trivial and time-consuming activities from your field of activities, and achieve your goals by prioritizing matters (based on importance, value, and urgency).

Let us not forget that if we do not know what is important to us and what is not important, we have lost valuable time. There is a whole lot of work to be done around all of the managers, and often the vision, insight, and time management fade in the clutter. Beware of the bad event that can disturb your growth and progress and challenge it.

PRIORITIES OF TIME

Tasks should be categorized and prioritized in a stepwise manner. A manager needs to know that specific tasks are a top priority. Like when you feel a sense of urgency or something that has quick returns and profitability. Also, something that contributes to the evolution of previous plans and other types of such transcendent matters. The best way to do things is to do things right, and this timely execution of work depends heavily on prioritizing time.

Tree pruning has many benefits, including better growth and return. As a tree has a lot of foliage, "time" also has a lot of foliage. By managing, prioritizing and trimming time, you actually increase profitability.

Keep in mind that time is full of benefit and profit. There are good opportunities in "time" and should be exploited quickly. Things that have a sooner and better return should be given top priority and those that are either low yielding or not yielding at all should be excluded. Missing useful and useless times is more common in the management field than in other social areas.

All capable managers acknowledge that more things that are important must be done at the earliest opportunity. Yet there are managers who do not have such understanding. One of the most interesting facts in the business and social relationship of executives is that they say: . . . we do not have time!

By claiming this, others think what an overcrowded manager they are that is deeply lost in the labyrinth of time! A manager who knows the time and priorities always has enough time.

Once, I had an appointment with a capable and punctual manager. He gave me an appointment three days after my call. When I went to his office as scheduled, he accepted me on time and refused to accept the clients and phone calls. (He believed it meant showing respect for the guest.) During the conversation, in response to why he gave me a three-day appointment after my call, he said:

- "I had much more urgent tasks. Much more urgent than conversation and interviewing. I had to take care of them."

That prioritizing by the executive was better than my meeting time appointment interfered with his chain meetings and his other matters, and neither could I be convinced nor could he handle his matters properly. For a capable manager, time is the first word in business. I dare say that profits and losses in a manager's business are highly time-dependent. The manager should extract useful times from his own and his organization's times.

More profit lies in useful times. Try to prioritize successfully. You must first identify what you want, know your plan, and write down your goals. Setting a goal and a plan does not mean you are deprived of other opportunities. Incidentally, this will help you identify the opportunities ahead. Setting a specific goal and plan helps you to have a clearer view of your ideal future. With this perspective, your vision is protected, your efforts are focused and your motivation will increase. A manager needs to prioritize according to the necessity. Robert Stevenson says:

- "Judge your day not with the product you harvest but with the seeds you plant."

Whenever you prioritize matters, you have actually planted a seed in the soil that will grow in the best possible way. Sporadic and dispersed matters will never have a good return. Just like seeds planted in poor soil with irregular irrigation.

PUNCTUALITY

We can talk about "time" a lot in order to clarify its significance. However, here is a brief discussion of it. An interesting thing in the community that is not far from the truth is that everyone is short of time!

If we look closely, we find that time shortage is due to instability in punctuality and failure to properly manage time. It is impossible for a punctual person to say: 'I have no time', even once. Because in the division of his working and daily hours, he has defined time for miscellaneous matters. Lack of time and shortage of time that most people in the community experience is due to their temporal disruption. Just like a newborn baby who has lost night and day.

I know a hairdresser who believes he has planned the best time division for himself! He sleeps until 11 o'clock in the morning!... Eats breakfast at 12 o'clock!... He leaves for his barbershop at about 1 pm. He works from 2 pm to 12 am. He returns home at 2 am and has dinner!... Many hairdressers are like that and interestingly, they justify such behavior.

I know a manager who comes to the office at noon and eats

breakfast! At 2 pm, he is full of energy, right at a time when the staff energy is exhausted and no one bothers to work. That time is just the beginning of his giving orders! Sometimes, he even keeps the staff up to 7 pm and stays in the workplace for up to 12 am! And this process is repeated, repeated and repeated ...

Such an unpunctual manager is constantly complaining about the current situation and work progress. What do you think is the cause of this turtle and snail movement of the organization?

Remember that "management" is at the top of everything. How would the staff feel if they see the manager's car in the parking lot before 8 am when they arrive at the workplace?

A tip, ... Some executives see "time" as a means to power! That is, they reduce their working hours and their presence. Because no one dares to question it! While one hour of the manager's absence is equal to one hour of the absence of each member of the staff. Now sum up the number of personnel and do the math.

Let's not forget that "killing time" does the most damage to an organization, and "punctuality" brings the most profit to an organization. A punctual manager will keep all the staff punctual.

This is an inherent characteristic of staff to spend more time on their own matters than on work! Hence, the statistics of daily and hourly leaves are terribly high.

So, keep in mind that the manager's waste of time and time instability will add up to the slow work progress, and this will be quickly propagated in the organization. If the staff were committed to their work as much as they are committed to their mandatory working hours, the company and the organization would have grown significantly.

A punctual manager actually knows how to take advantage of his time and how to make the most of the opportunities when the staff is available to him. A leading and successful manager knows six things well:

Himself - his work - his time – people around him - his staff - his goals.

Punctual people waste the least amount of time. Therefore, they are less likely to have overdue work. Punctual people are valuable people. Because they value their most valuable asset. For a manager, several factors lead to his attraction and influence on the organization. Including:

Commitment, discipline, punctuality.

The personnel monitors the actions and behavior of the manager more than the manager scrutinizing them does. Just like a school principal that all students know, see and recognize his attributes. While the principal himself does not know and will not know half of his students.

No matter how much a manager earns or what situation he is going through, the important thing is to get the job done properly. A punctual manager, if he notices it would take less than a few minutes to complete the next acti

on, will promptly do so.

Dear manager!

Disengage yourself from daily routines that waste your time and energy, so you can focus on more important tasks with a greater return.

The End

www.ingramcontent.com/pod-product-compliance
Lightning Source LLC
Chambersburg PA
CBHW061638040426
42446CB00010B/1470